SPIRITUAL MISFITS

Collaboration and Belonging in a Divisive World

SHAHAR RABI, PH.D.

Printed in the United States of America
First Printing, 2019

ISBN-13: 978-0-9813703-4-7

CONTENTS

Emptiness gave birth to form.
Form came alive.
Life evolved, and asked,
Who am I?

Orient yourself to the question
that holds all of the answers to come.
For the benefit of all beings,
And of the planet

And that which wants to know.

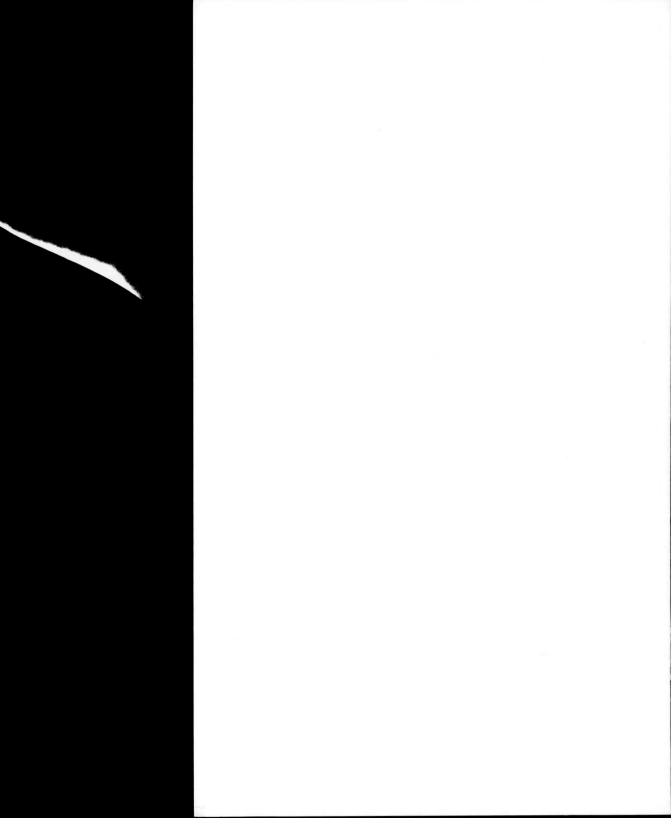

ACKNOWLEDGMENTS

This book is a footnote to a long legacy of brilliant minds and awakened beings that came before.[1] The list is long. It includes eastern and western philosophers and psychologists, as well as the great religious and spiritual traditions. Every encounter I have had with this vast territory has molded what I am sharing. They are the ingredients of the dish I have prepared for you. I have added salt and pepper, for taste, and cooked it (well, I hope!), but I cannot claim ownership of the ingredients from which this dish was made.

The work of Ken Wilber has its footprints all over this book. His integral map, with its quadrants, stages, and states, has had a profound impact on my thinking. Carl Jung inspired me to embrace mystery and not to be afraid to follow my intuition. The writings of Simone Weil inspired me to fall in love with God again, and Jiddu Krishnamurti invited me to question everything. Carl Graves (through Dr. Don Beck) gave me spiral dynamics as a lens through which to understand human and social development, and the inspired philosophical writings of Jacob Needleman encouraged me that there is some merit to my ideas. Lama Mark Webber reminded me about the profound value of spiritual depth, lineage, and tradition. The writings of Anodea Judith spoke to the value of both east and west. Lastly, Pierre Teilhard de Chardin offered a vision of an evolving God, which made me believe that religion and science can coexist.

I also would like to also thank my wife, Saskia Tait, for her ongoing active support and amazing editorial skills; Jan Tiz, for our enlightening dialogue; Tina Overbury for teaching me how to listen; Meribeth Deen for her caring edits; and Richard Labonté, for his editorial fine-tuning. Special thanks to Josh Colman, for believing in me; Dr. Asa-Sophia Maglio and the counselling team at Adler University for the support; Jane Tubinshlak for the original model design, Lorinda Strang for her leadership, Elaine Taylor for her support, Amihay Zelinkovsky for our friendship and Chris Dierkes for the feedback. Lastly, a big thank you to x-pod, and the women of "fight club" for being my first attempts at a 'religion without a religion.'

In memory of
Bridget
Cowie

—

I promise you three things:
I will not try to convert,
fix or change you.

You are needed just as you are.
I only ask that you lean into the edges of yourself.
I will meet you on the other side.

A NEW STORY

This book is a new, more inclusive story of who we can become. Not the true story, the only story, or even the best story. It is a new story because it is still unborn and, if you choose, you will carry and birth it together with others.

You.

The misfit.

The one who is finished with business as usual.

You are not a rebel. Rebels react. You are not from the resistance because you are a part of the problem. You are not defined by your past, but you embrace it. You know how desperately we need new stories about who we are, why we are here, and what we should do... what we *can* do... to ensure that our planet will be habitable in years to come. You are aligned with a core story that *every* single person and *each* point of view matters. But you also sense that holding (only) this story is no longer valid—our stories need to synch. Like a guitar chord, each story is a note that can be played simultaneously, to create new harmonies. Ideas, feelings and experiences can be woven into larger stories about how we can come together, learn from each other, heal, and love. You know that collaboration is possible, even among enemies.

You sense that it is no longer acceptable to just agree to disagree, or to assume that because our stories are different, they are incompatible. All of *these* stories are also outdated because they do not take into consideration how complex we have become and how we need stories that can bridge and fuse the growing fragmentation in society.

I want to make stories that dare not to know their endings, that help us understand our interdependence and to rethink our outlooks on life. I want to take part in creating stories where paradoxes are accepted, mystery is celebrated, and soulful living is integrated, with everyday practicalities. Stories that do not sacrifice human needs on the alter of cultural and social values.

In these stories, we are the protagonists and the supporting cast, the writers and the fictional characters. These stories are not random, and they do not resolve neatly. They combine playful chaos with harmony, the rhythms of life with the inherent balance of the universe, systemic thinking with radical acceptance.

Our lives are the ink with which
these stories will be told.

Our stories are always part of a bigger story, which is itself part of an even larger, always evolving story. No matter how truthful your story is, it is partial. This is also true of the stories I will tell in this book, and of your reaction to them. In my own life, I have sometimes felt resistance to change when someone offered me a perspective that was different from my own. The hardest thing to do is to admit to ourselves that we are wrong or limited when the perspectives that we hold so dearly no longer align with the ever-dynamic nature of reality.

You see, humans have the innate capacity to adapt to new environments, ideas, and values. But we also have an inherent fear of change. Once in a while, this tension facilitates a massive shift in how we live and perceive the world. For example, the 17th century gave us the Age of Enlightenment, a radical shift that made *reason* the dominant form of thinking and introduced such concepts as liberty, science, and tolerance. The first part of the 20th century brought humanism and then relativism. The second part of the 20th century saw an explosion of knowledge and access to technology we couldn't have dreamed of before.[2] I believe we are ready for another big shift—a call to adapt— by integrating all that came before with what we know today, for the sake of a sustainable future.

It is the contention of this book that premodern wisdom

can coexist with modern ideals *and* postmodern freedom. Throughout the past 300 years, we have divided everything into many wonderfully discrete systems, but have not done enough to integrate them into working synergies, especially in the domain of spirituality and psychotherapy. This division should be seen not as an endgame but a stepping stone in the evolution of our collective spiritual work.

It is happening. With each passing year, momentum toward integration is building. We can, through what can only be understood as new emerging stories, heal the ancestral wounds in our communities for the benefit of people and life on this planet.

We need new types of synergies that can simultaneously grasp the incredible diversity we hold as a species, together with localized, *human scale,* collaborations. Far too many of us are isolated in this respect. Torn between our human potential (and need) to actualize as individuals and the lingering thirst for what can only be realized by commitment to a system that is bigger than the self.

If you are a seeker of this kind of integration, this book is for you. If you feel like a misfit in a confused world, this book is for you. If you seek more collaboration and belonging, this book is for you! It will speak to your longing for depth but also to the reason you cannot go back to your original spiritual home—no matter how profound, wise, or complete it may be.

Because you are from more than
just one world(view).

You seek a common ground among differences and the emergence of new ways of perception. You hold a vision for the future, but still do not know how to make it come alive *today* for yourself and for the people and planet you care about.

You live in the future.
Surrounded by the past.

There is a reason you feel this way: You see that the solutions currently on offer will not suffice: The ideas of today cannot address the needs of tomorrow. You are not alone. There are many like you. I meet them daily in my community, in my office, at gatherings I host, and when I teach. They are parents, ecologists, politicians, spiritual leaders, educators, researchers, students, and economists. Each might come to this from a different perspective, but like you, they have all felt a call to adapt.

And all of them agree that we must reorient our thinking about the issues at hand. This reorientation will need structure to thrive because insights happen in context. They need to be cultivated by organizations, culture, and social systems. And how can the insights of tomorrow be born in a collective psyche that produces structures that still run on high amounts of fear, exclusion, and dual thinking?

What is called for is an upgrade to our cultural operating system.

This is true in fields as diverse as education, science, politics, and spirituality. And it is happening already in some profound ways around the world. Just not fast enough. Despite the fact that my interests range across all of these fields, I chose to focus this book on the role that spiritual misfits (that's you—you would not pick up this book if you were not one) will play in co-creating the future of western spirituality.

If you sense the tectonic shifts in the geopolitical atmosphere around the world; if you discern how social media and the internet at large are contributing to epidemics of loneliness and isolation; and if you do not know what to do, then you are ready to start the difficult work of dialoguing with the unknown. Because of your inherent flexibility and capacity to be at ease with multiple perspectives, you are in a unique position to facilitate the kind of conversations that will give rise to new, more expansive stories.

My offer is modest. It is not a grand theory, but rather a model for *grassroots* solutions that can shield your immediate circle of family, friends, and community from the impact of what is to come. The model I present might feel like a tiny dinghy facing rogue waves of unwieldy, unpredictable events, but it is more than that. It is a much-needed cultural counter to heightened individuality on the one hand and to ethnocentricity on the other. I see it as the next stage in post-secular spiritual engagement.

My model is open source, flexible, and simple to use, and is based on many years of personal and academic research, including facilitating spiritual and therapeutic groups in Canada and in other countries. The model is like a story factory: you can weave in meta-narratives that speak to *your* community and embrace your personal ones. It is designed to mimic forces of nature that have sprung from the source itself (which I call God, but please call it whatever you want). It will allow you to integrate wisdom traditions, science, and postmodern choice in the interest of greater collaboration and belonging.

You do not need to read this book from cover to cover. Each chapter was written to stand alone. To help you make the most of the model, I have divided this book into two parts. **Part One** offers the rationale and context for the model. In it, you will find three sections, representing three contextual aspects of the misfit's mission: Spiritual, religious and social. These sections will speak differently to different people. **Part Two** describes in more detail how the model might be used in your community and give you a blueprint of a working model. In the end of Part two, you will find a chapter on the dangers of spiritual collaboration. I encourage you to not skip that chapter.

If you are less interested in the overview Part One provides, you can skip to Part Two to learn how to implement the model in your life and in your community and go back to Part One later, as needed, to dive into the context and theory.

I want you to think of this book as an invitation to inhabit a way of being that aligns with life's intelligence, however you define that intelligence. It is a weaving that provides the capacity to see beyond your current social, cultural, and spiritual horizons. I believe that this is one of the central tasks of our time and that this is what is being asked of 'misfits'.

We live in a truly uncommon age of integration. Vast amounts of knowledge are being organized and integrated in ground-breaking, systematic ways.[3] All over the world, people are creating revolutionary models of spiritual, psychological, ecological, and cultural ways of operating, all trying to provide solutions to our current local and global crises. These are bridges to a worldview that many are sensing is coming—one where truth can be universal, relative, and developmental *all at once*. Each generation has an opportunity to participate in the creative, co-evolutionary unfolding of reality. Now it is our turn.

PART
ONE

SPIRITUAL
CONTEXT

*Where I explain what a spiritual misfit is
and how I heard the call to action.*

B̲efore you read this part, I want you to try something.

Pretend we do not speak the same language. The words will *seem* the same, but they have different meanings to you and to me.

There are two reasons for this exercise:

First, I am an immigrant. I swim in the kiddie pool of English, while you get to dive in the deep end. So, the ways in which I express and translate my ideas are limited.

Second, we all live in different psycho-social realities. Any word—let alone charged words like *love*, *God*, or *religion*—evokes unique associations for every individual.

This little imaginative experiment demonstrates how we are all held captive by the limits of our own minds.

Let's try not to get lost in translation.

1 | ON BEING A MISFIT

*You matter to life. Without you, life
misses a beat—your life.
Remember, you have been here as matter
from the beginning.
Please take time and take space. Because
you matter to us.*

I used to think that if I were more committed
or less proud, I would be fully engaged in an established
religious tradition. Oh, how I longed to belong. To surrender
to a truth and finally arrive. I thought that if I just *let go* of
what I knew from my years of training as an educator and
psychotherapist and instead *believed*, I could make life work
better for myself and my family. It's not that I didn't try.

I grew up Jewish, fell in love with Christianity, practiced
Buddhism for many years, and devotedly practiced and
eventually taught both yoga and meditation. I used to say
that my mind is Jewish, my heart is Christian, my body is
Hindu, and my being is Buddhist. These are just silly labels,
I know, but they mark traditions and practices that harbor
profound depths and beauty. Contemplating and embodying
their wisdom has been central to my spiritual journey.

As a spiritual explorer, I spent most of my twenties learning from great masters in Israel, Canada, the U.S., India, Thailand, and Nepal. I tried to become a monk and traveled in India for two years, learning from awakened masters and incredible teachers. I joined eccentric groups, practiced Vipassana a few times and even wrote a Master's thesis on its benefits. I ingested ayahuasca and mushrooms and explored whatever spiritual teachings I could get my hands on. I felt the joy of belonging and the excitement of learning, and I touched depths of spiritual wisdom along each pathway.

All of these experiences changed me for the better. I went from being a somewhat selfish, dissociative, and fearful person, to somebody one might describe as being reasonably loving, present, and courageous. Ultimately, however, I encountered a certain rigidity in every tradition, which stopped me from dedicating the rest of my life to any one path. No matter how profound, awake, intelligent, or wise the teacher was (and some blew my mind right open), there always came a moment where they would reject a well-researched psychological concept or a commonly accepted scientific truth, or where they exhibited a bias against other cultures or traditions.

I remember being part of a non-dual community in India where one of the lead teachers instructed me to stop reading books from or about other traditions and to focus only on that community's texts. I remember being baffled by that request. How could they not see that what they were teaching was influenced by other traditions? How could it be that this person, who was clearly awakened and intelligent, felt threatened by other traditions and communities of practice? I also recall interviewing a famous rabbi, wondering if his religious school would be a good place for me. He kept mocking Christianity while we spoke. Here again, I found a teacher who could not find depth or beauty in teachings of another faith, spoken perhaps in a different language.

While visiting spiritual communities, I discovered a certain smugness in those who had bought in to the ideas of their tradition. They had an air of authority born from a conviction that their path was the right one, and they seemed to harbor the assumption that all would be well with the world if everybody would see what they saw. I experienced something similar to this in academia as well, especially when I tried to express spiritual worldviews to my scientific and atheistic friends.

All of these experiences fueled my curiosity. I had a sense that each view was true, but partial. I saw the validity in opposite perspectives and the partiality in all points of view. These experiences, and my own smugness when engulfed in a teaching, helped me to understand how limited and counterproductive these attitudes are at a time when what we need most is mutual understanding and greater collaboration.

On the other end of the spectrum were traditions so open, inclusive and non-hierarchical that I could not find a clear voice, a sense of identity and boundary. These countless contemporary maps promised to provide new answers. As progressive and open-minded as they seemed, I noticed a lack of awareness sometimes manifesting as insensitivity or even harshness to the subtleties of psychological, spiritual, and cultural needs.

In these type of spiritual groups, I could not find organized and well-established sets of practices, ceremonies, and initiations that could lead a practitioner to both psychological maturation and spiritual awakening without sensing that I now belonged to a cult. So, there I was. Stuck in the middle between too much and too little. I wondered:

Should I choose to dedicate my life to mastering one tradition *or* should I retain the freedom to pick and choose from countless perspectives in the spiritual marketplace? (Mastery vs. diversity).

Should I pledge my allegiance to one spiritual group and thereby resolve my need to belong, *or* should I stay on the path of the hero's journey? (Group vs. individuation).

Is the world a display of countless points of view that are all equal in value and importance, *or* do some spiritual views have more *objective* validity than others? (Hierarchy vs. pluralism).

Little did I know it would be another eight years before I found a satisfying answer to these questions. What I found was that I did not have to have to choose, and that in doing so I was making the right choice.

Let me explain. It is hard to suspend what you know in order to get what you want. It's like being in a relationship with someone you know is not good for you, but staying because it's comfortable or less frightening than being alone or facing the world of dating. For me to truly commit to one tradition, group, or perspective, I would have had to erase or subdue parts of myself, turn a blind eye to scientific truths, and/or let go of moral and ethical stances that I knew to be important. As it stood, the price was too high.

So, I became a spiritual misfit. Someone searching for a spiritual home that hasn't been built yet. Of course, I had my practices, insights, and inspiring teachers, but I needed more. Not because my spiritual path was lacking in value but because I knew my personal story was a fraction of the great (and graceful) unfolding of reality. In short, I knew I needed to be of service to what I understood as the emerging collective experience.

With time, I came to understand the critical importance of being a spiritual misfit. Who I am (and who I believe we all are) is an impulse to evolve, develop, and adapt; to not only discover but also to create something from nothing. Even if I had embraced the whole package of a single tradition, it would not have been enough. I was not able to compromise because something inside of me sensed a future that was still in the imagination of God, and that I and others would play a role in making it a reality.

And before you freak out, please do not take what I'm saying here literally. For me, the imagination of God is a metaphor for the source of creative solutions that we have used so many times before. It is the place of hope, change, and grace, whether or not you want to use the word God.

So I invite you to stay open. But *really* open, because once you are open to your role, you will notice that underneath your self-protective layers, there is a heart that serves life (which includes you). And only from there will you find the bliss and love that you already are.

But life kept happening. I fell in love. My spiritual intensity morphed to relational passion and the journey of spirit took a more earthly twist. I got married, immigrated to Canada, and eventually had two wonderful children. The spiritual adventures of my twenties gave way to family life. The nagging feeling of needing to belong was finally met through the love I found in, and that I have, for my family. The spiritual burn cooled. Then, about four years ago, it came back. With a vengeance...

THE CALL

I know exactly the moment it happened. The place on the walk. A flash. A call for action from within. It was a request: Create a space to celebrate ever-evolving reality rooted in *community*. Yes, *celebrate:* have fun, play, experience joy, relax... because *you are* that ever-evolving reality that has always been implanted in community.

This call was an invitation to build a container—for what exactly, I did not know. The call was woefully short on details. My first response? "Sounds great, but I am busy." A few months later, the call came again. This time I knew I needed to do something. I was burning out at work. My old-time bestie, depression, was rearing its ugly head. My grounded-vulnerable self was giving way to a prickly-grumpy self. I was not paying attention and I was paying a price.

So, I took time away from work for a one-month solo meditation retreat. What I heard was clear—follow the impulse. Find answers. I started speaking to leaders in the field, writing, and meditating to figure out how I could manifest the call practically.

Before I go any further with my story, I want to make three important points: First, the voice was not speaking to me specifically. I was not *chosen* (no one is). Rather, I believe that I heard an open call that anybody can tune in to. It is a call for action that I know so many of you also hear, and it had nothing to do with any specific religion or unique set of gifts. Second, I believe that the space I was asked to build does need not be a physical location. It can also be a state of mind that lives in the space between people and perspectives. Third, it is not my intention to create a new theory. There are plenty of good ones out there already. Instead, I decided that I could best serve by offering a structure that anyone who heard this call could embrace.

This experience was terrifying, in part because it asked me to publicly state that I want to serve something that many do not care about, or worse despise—i.e., God. I did not want to be pigeonholed by religious or non-religious groups. But neither did I want to hide anymore.

I believe that the story of God, the future of God, is being written by us whether we choose to participate in creating it or not.

Initially, I answered the call by playing around with different concepts and ideas. However, all of my early prototypes failed to integrate or address the subtleties of the original call. I was certain that people who hold premodern, modern, and postmodern worldviews could collaborate. I knew it was the key to moving culture forward, but I did not understand how to make it work. I had to do some serious additional digging. Soon, my passion project took center stage in my life.

In retrospect, I was naive to believe that I could find elemental patterns that would answer my questions. The task was daunting and I did not have a clue where to start. Luckily, I was not alone. The more I researched, the more I understood that my insights were overlapping with established ideas of the 20th and 21st centuries.

From Carl Jung's theory of the Self to Ken Wilber's integral theory (and so many in between)—they all added critical perspectives that eventually became the basis for the working model I call the Comprehensive Orientation for Developmental Emergence. The CODE (which is elaborated on in Part Two) is a modular, open-source, and adaptable framework for collaborative spirituality.

Before we go any further, let me break it down: *Comprehensive* in this context means to include as many perspectives and tools as needed. Community building is hard work and it's much harder when the community is highly diverse or when a group of very strong individuals try to collaborate spiritually, without a leader. Having a comprehensive mind means that a community can lean into many perspectives in their collaborative work. The five guiding principles of the CODE can be a great starting point, but in the end, it is the role of the community to seek an ever-expansive understanding of its worldview and values. This can be likened to being nourished by a well-balanced and diverse diet.

Orientation is about having a *direction*. Toward what? More joy, more peace, more collaboration, more growth. In other words, the fulfillment of peoples' core needs, but equally important (in this model), the potential of post-secular collaborative work in an age of fragmentation and individuation. Orientation is the ability to lean, together with others, into open-ended questions, and to discover the insights that can only be found in spiritual collaboration. Think about Orientation as your (value based) compass.

The *developmental* aspect of the CODE is just that—to know where each person is developmentally at any given moment, and to be respectful of that. People and groups are developmental entities and therefore need appropriate (developmental) engagement. Pushing too hard toward collaborative work or holding a common goal can be detrimental for the health of the community. This is why in this model, safety always comes first. This can be likened to a workout at the gym: push too hard and you will hurt yourself, but if you don't push hard enough you won't accomplish anything.

Lastly, the model is an *Emerging* process and not a means to an end. There are no long-term goals, nor is there a destination. Instead, an alignment with the emerging qualities of the now is what propels the process. Think about this as if you are a collaborative artist in dialogue with your art, and in this case, the art is in the creation of the community.

In simple terms, the CODE is a framework for collaboration in situations where complexity is high and tolerance has the potential to be low. And as we know, spiritual ideals and cultural belief systems are known to be of the latter sort.

I offer this model as a *starting point* for a much-needed conversation within and among the great traditions. Once explained, you will be able to use it for your family, in your established tradition, and as a way to collaborate with and learn from different spiritual beliefs, even among agnostic, new age, and non-religious groups.

However, the main purpose of the CODE is to offer a simple structure for the work of integration and healing among misfits. Misfits, who yearn to bring their fullest selves to relationships that are in search of the expanding stories of our time. Because all stories matter.

Not only on their own, but because they matter to each other. By hearing other stories, we understand our own better *and* can share the story of our humanity with others. As spirit, culture, and people evolve, so should the structures that hold us and sustain life. Thus, each generation is asked to creatively participate as embedded *interpreters* in the collaborative, evolutionary unfolding of reality.

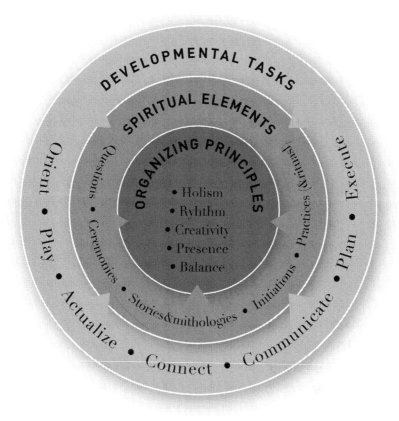

DEVELOPMENTAL TASKS	SPIRITUAL ELEMENTS	ORGANIZING PRINCIPLES
Orient: Engage from safety.	Practices (and rituals)	**Holism:** The great way (Antidote to isolation)
Play: Orient from pleasure. Lean into safety.	Questions	
Actualize: Play with agency. Lean into pleasure	Ceremonies	**Rhythm:** The pulse of life (Antidote to dysregulation)
Connect: Actualize love. Lean into agency	Initiations (and rights of passage)	**Creativity:** When everything goes (Antidote for fear)
Communicate: Connect to Communicate. Lean into love.	Stories and mythologies	**Presence:** Tapping into what is already perfect (Antidote to suffering)
Plan: Communicate your common vision. Lean into communication.		**Balance:** 'Yes, no and maybe…?' (Antidote to rigidity)
Execute: Plan your action. Lean into vision.		

THE CODE – A FIRST GLANCE

As you can see in the model, the CODE is based on five organizing principles, five spiritual elements, and seven developmental tasks. The *five organizing principles* can be understood as the container that keeps you aligned in each step of the process. The *five spiritual elements* are what makes the process come alive. *The developmental aspect* of the CODE is the operational framework for the process. It builds the psychological condition for maximizing your potential as a human. All these terms will become clear after reading Part two.

You can think of the CODE as an approach that encompasses what I term 'deep-diversity'— A system thinking approach to diversity that simultaneously provides depth, developmental theory and inclusivity, in the interest of developing innovative integrations that redefine who we are as carriers of life. My hope is that the schism and fragmentation between religions, between religions and science, and between modernism and postmodernism can be mended by the principles, elements, and processes of the CODE.

Thus, this model is not an abandonment of the individual project[4] in favour of a group one, nor is it a regression into older religious forms. It is also not simply a buffet of new-age, spiritual beliefs. To paraphrase the work of the French philosopher François Laruelle, what I heard that afternoon in the meadow was a call to co-author new *nonstandard religions* or *non-religious religions*.[5]

An evolutionary leap,
into all that came before,
for the sake of what is about to come.

I use the plural religion(s) and not singular religion because in my story of the future, we will see countless micro-religions emerging. They will be based on growing dialogues between existing religions, fused with science and contemporary thinking. These nonstandard religions will include systems thinking, ecological perspectives, scientific inquiry, psychology, and sociocultural insight and critique. They will come in endless variety, inspired by local visions and wisdom, and they will have the capacity to be flexible enough to incorporate different perspectives without collapsing into relativism.

A growing number of people and organizations around the world are beginning to have these kinds of conversations. Spiritual misfits everywhere are picking up on the call for action. Multi-faith and evolutionary churches are popping up everywhere. Books, conferences, academic programs and thrilling new religious concepts are being launched. A newly emergent worldview is being explored, experimented with, and practiced. These are the signs that there is a longing for a new wave of *relating* and *belonging*, weaving of self with others, past and present, into new patterns of spiritual collaboration previously unrealized.

Nobody, myself included, has any idea how this model will play out in your community—what answers you will find, or how it will feel. I don't even know if you'll be using the terms God or religion, spirituality, or evolution. Truth be told, I don't care, as long as you accept that you have a part to play in life's unfolding and give room for what (I believe) is one of the most important reason you are alive: to consciously participate in improving and sustaining life on this planet.

The CODE is open-source and local. What makes the model distinctive is the fact that it offers practical structures that you can use in your own community. Each community and group has complete autonomy with regards to how to engage it. As such, you are welcome to ignore any of the ideas I share in the book, and just use the model as a kind of open-source code.

It builds safety and trust. If communities are to thrive spiritually and psychologically, we need to create containers that are small enough that people can feel safe to share and explore their needs, values, concerns, and questions. People need spaces where they can feel safe to be vulnerable, and thus more attached, to others. My extensive research on developmental psychology has shown that without this fundamental sense of security, individuals will not feel comfortable to learn and grow in ways that go beyond intellectual or spiritual understanding. I have also ensured that the model supports the development of clear boundaries among members.

It respects both authentic spiritual lineages and science. The world's religious and spiritual traditions have mapped the human psyche, each in their unique (and limited) ways. This is not something you can absorb during a weekend-long retreat, through YouTube tutorials, or by reading books. The CODE encourages people to embrace one (or more) lineages for the establishment of depth. For me, lineages include any one of the great authentic religions but also Western psychological knowledge and scientific dialectics.[6]

It is about self and others. It isn't enough to just have an intellectual conversation or to exchange spiritual ideas. People deserve more. In fact, they *need* more. They need a space where the self, others, and the divine force that unites them are all active participants in an open-ended, self-reflective process. I want people to have an experience where everyone has a chance to be their best selves emotionally, spiritually, and intellectually while growing the relational art of meeting *otherness*.

It brings the best of all worlds. People sense that they need to make an unnecessary choice between different aspects of who they are. Can they be both spiritual and scientific? Religious and rational? Can they live in multiple identities? The CODE offers a process in which nothing has to be given up and nothing needs to be changed. To use a metaphor, our cultural RAM (RAM being the capacity to run multiple computer applications at once) has enough processing power to handle the paradoxes of our time. Each community has differentiated and stand-alone spiritual traditions, diverse groups, *and* the common ground of the group that unifies it all. This is not only multiculturalism in action but the embrace of the full spectrum of developmental spirit.

It is developmental. The CODE taps into the dynamic nature of human development on the individual, community, and cultural levels. This developmental process is critical because achieving our fullest development requires that we attend to any unfinished developmental tasks remaining from childhood or adolescence. Lingering unmet needs create psychosocial disturbances for individuals and the people they interact with. Poorly managed developmental trauma can wreak havoc in the lives of individuals, partnerships, families, and communities. This is why so many well-intended spiritual groups and religious organizations go through excruciating growing pains. It is also why the first task of any group working with the CODE will be to help its members to orient, find ground, and feel safe. Many groups skip this step and eventually find themselves stuck. This, in turn, creates a false sense of security in the community. Other communities skip straight to focusing on their vision and sacrificing the need for individuation for the sake of a bigger collective vision.

The CODE was my answer to the call I heard years ago. It was why I could not choose only one path. It is why you might find it hard to choose one tradition or go back to *your* cultural roots. It is why some of us feel like misfits.

FROM ME AND WE

During my research, I was completely absorbed by the ideas that would become this book: *evolving God*, *spiritual misfits*, and the *future of religion*. I consulted with Jewish rabbis, Christian ministers, and Buddhist lamas. I also dialogued with people who had consciously chosen to leave organized religion. I wanted to understand how they would relate to my ideas and how they saw the future of religion and spirituality. Our conversations about co-authoring the future generated a sense of optimism and excitement in me. So many of the people I spoke with saw the importance of these topics.

In addition to my ongoing talks with spiritual leaders, I also organized conversations in my community. I called the first set of conversations *The Future of God* and the second *The Age of Integration*. I was pleasantly surprised to discover that so many members of the small community where I live had an interest in these subjects.

Along with an excitement about sharing experiences, ideas, and perspectives, there was also frustration, anger, and grief expressed in connection with religion. One person was so furious about the religion of his upbringing that I worried he might have a heart attack when he spoke! Another person refused to use the word "religion," and another insisted that we are "all one" no matter how different we are. *Group members seemed to get stuck, unable to move beyond exhibiting respect to finding a common ground in a meaningful way.*

This was frustrating because it was clear that people wanted to connect and belong, but could not. The diversity of perspectives and worldviews in the room threatened to make consensus impossible. The dialogue fluctuated between, at best, being pleasant and inspiring and, at worst, being divisive or just boring. Sometimes, people simply shared their pre-rehearsed ideas, as opposed to engaging in the conversation that was alive in the room.

Emerging from these conversations, I found the essence of my work. I learned why I identify as a misfit and why so many people I encountered can't find their spiritual home.

This was not an issue of people not getting along, but of limited updated frames of thought and effective structures.

Think about it. We are living at a time fraught with challenge and simultaneously ripe with promise. We possess considerable socio-cultural and historical knowledge and have a higher tolerance for cultural diversity than ever before. Our world is exploding with perspectives, and yet at the same time people find it hard to sustain deep, heartfelt spiritual and psychological connections. We just don't have spiritual, political, or cultural models that demonstrate that it is possible to manage incredible diversity and complexity *while at the same time* producing collaboration and a sense of belonging.

We are spiritual misfits for a reason. Like nomads seeking a new *psychological and spiritual* promised land, we are called to travel to unfamiliar places to seek a better future.

The Story of Abraham comes to my mind. The Lord says to Abraham, "Leave your land, your family, and your father's household for the land that I will show you." God asks Abraham to be dislocated for the rest of his life—not only to leave his land and his relatives, but also his culture and past beliefs. Abraham's journey was an act of total trust in an inner voice. He had to forsake all that was known for an unknown future. This is akin to leaping off the edge of the world only to discover you have wings. Remarkably, there are fables of people making this kind of courageous leap throughout history.

The suffering in our tormented world today indicates for some that it is time to take this kind of metaphorical leap. We must be willing to push past the comfort and boundaries of our worldviews towards a creative and expansive vision of the future. Like Abraham, we can walk from our inner lands and cultural heritage into uncharted territories of the creative impulse...or God. I believe we can offer our children, and the earth a new kind of vision. One with multiple promised lands of reverence that are alive, safe, diverse, loving, expressive, visionary, and whole. Spiritual misfits everywhere are being invited to follow a call that will birth a place beyond hope and fear.

A NEW KIND OF *US*

In some respects, my family is a good example of multiculturalism and pluralism. We celebrate Christmas and the Jewish holidays. We attend Buddhist retreats, and my wife owned a yoga studio where she regularly invited speakers representing multiple faiths and perspectives on spirituality. We both wrote doctoral dissertations focused on East-West psychology and spirituality. Our children are learning about many manifestations of the divine through books, songs, and stories.

Other families all around us seem to offer different versions of this, arising from their respective cultural backgrounds and spiritual interests. I think of all of these families as inventors of micro-spiritual traditions, floating in a sea of fragmented perspectives. Respectful and isolated. Many of the families I speak to wish to engage in collaborative spirituality, but without the coercive demands and expectations imposed by some premodern or modern religious structures.

I love my children very much and want the best for them. I want them to play, develop, and mature to become resilient adults who are proud of themselves and of what they contribute to their communities. I believe that having a contemplative lifestyle will help them to develop into this kind of person. My wife and I do our best to provide them with a psychological, cultural, and spiritual context that is relevant to their lineage, culture, and surroundings. In other words, we are doing our best to provide our kids with a cultural and spiritual grounding that will sustain them in the years to come. Nevertheless, I can't help but feel that something is missing. As a child, I was nourished and sustained by a highly cohesive and ethnocentric culture. I knew who I was, what was expected of me, how to understand the world around me, and who was *in* and who was *out* of our cultural circles. Growing up, I had no idea how dramatically this milieu contributed to making me the man I am today.

So, when I think about what is missing in my current life as a Canadian, I reflect on a childhood defined by the rhythms of my native culture and place of birth—the quiet streets on Yom Kippur, the feeling of Shabbat with the sounds of children playing and families walking. Even in chaotic and sometimes disorganized moments of my life growing up, the seasons provided a pulse and my culture provided a sense of grounding.

When I consider the future, I worry about what lies ahead for my children and for generations to come with regard to spiritual nourishment. What meaning will they make of their life? Who they will seek for spiritual support? How will they know what to trust as valid and life-giving? Will they have spiritual insight to lean on in the unavoidable tough moments they will experience?

Like it or hate it, there is something compelling in meeting religious people who have clear answers about how to live their lives. I worry that my children are missing out on something I took for granted: A coherent and clear map of how the world works. I know that I cannot provide them with what I once had. There is no way an individual like myself can provide the sense of belonging and cultural depth that I experienced by osmosis through the world I was raised in.

On the one hand, my children live in one of the most progressive countries, with one of the most tolerant cultures in the world. They can choose to be, think, and do whatever they want, as long as they do not hurt others and obey the law. This is truly incredible and speaks to the enormous achievements of Canada.

On the other hand, this freedom comes with a price. They do not belong to a spiritual structure that is larger than just our family because we don't fit into any one religious structure. In a way, they are bounded by their existential freedom and choice. They have to walk their own path with little religious context.

Sadly, my wife and I can't go back to our original spiritual homes. We have both been exposed to so many other traditions and ways that we know that no single approach can suffice. Our spiritual journeys are still very much personal — we respect each other's paths and do our best to encourage curiosity in our children. But despite all of this, a common ground that extends *beyond* our family is missing.

This spiritual isolation is a choice, but I sense it is also something more. We don't have enough choices, we lack updated religious models that can offer us not just diversity of spiritual perspectives, but new formations of spiritual collaboration among people and families. This is a missing link that needs to be addressed. We need a new collaborative spiritual structures and adaptive forms of religion.

I believe that the future of religion will allow an "us" that can have it all — we won't have to feel like spiritual misfits any longer. All of life's threads will be welcomed.

What I am pointing to is not another iteration of pluralism or multiculturalism. These are important, but they are *limited* in their capacity to hold both deep-diversity and depth. At the core of their philosophy lies a problematic assumption that prevents the expansion of our understanding of God and religion. I will say much more about this in chapters that follow, but for now it is important that you understand that I am not simply talking about respecting, honoring, or learning from diverse traditions. Rather, I am talking about developing new, coherent spiritual projects that express the unique impulse of our time. Structures that can help to transcend our personal boundaries to meet others in *and* through mutual experience — where I create you and you create me, and together we create a new *us*.

This is a radically new act of diversity at the edge of culture.

I like to compare our embrace of cultural *diversity* to the technological triumphs of the past few decades, such as personal computers, digital cameras, and email. *Synergy* is different. *Synergy* was the moment when Steve Jobs launched the first smartphone. He took each and every technological triumph (phone, camera, internet, representing diversity) and integrated them into one device. The Iphone is the perfect example of what I call synergy. Through this merging of technologies,, Apple created something so revolutionary that it has fundamentally and profoundly changed the way we work, play, and connect. Technological diversity became technological synergy, and the world has not looked back.

I believe the next step of the human integration will involve a similar kind of synergistic leap. Diverse worldviews will become integrated and localized, cooperative forms of spirituality that are radically original will emerge, teaching a broader *context*:

> *A context that goes beyond personal spirituality.*
> *Beyond traditions and religions.*
> *Beyond worldviews.*
> *Beyond new theoretical frameworks.*[7]
> *It will not provide answers.*
> *But weave the old and the new,*
> *The heart of religions,*
> *With the future.*
> *Flexible and humble to know*
> *It can never be complete.*

These new kind of collaborations will express the same living impulse that was present at the moment of creation so many billions of years ago, and it is the same *impulse* that will show us what needs to be done next.

2 | THE IMPULSE

All that you touch, you change.

All that you change, changes you.

The only lasting truth is change.

God is change (Octavia Butler)

There is an impulse. Nature abides by it. Life flows from it. Poets attempt to describe it. Scientists observe it. The impulse is a cross-cultural and *developmental* phenomenon. Its basic qualities appear in all cultures throughout history, although they manifest differently due to its adaptable and creative nature. The impulse is *alive* and is thus always changing. Like waves and particles, it escapes definition (as a wave) and yet, we always and inevitably embody it (as a particle, when we give it our awareness).

The impulse is a call of love to all that is sacred in the Cosmos. It is the past and future, arising in the now. Always evolving, self-organizing, unifying, it includes everything that came before you. It is the sum total of all that is and all that will be.

It keeps reinventing itself to discover more of itself. You

know it most directly when you sense the miracle that you are— where you might have come from, where you are heading as a person, as part of the zeitgeist, and as part of the story of humanity.

You are a child of the Cosmos. The one and only you; there will never be another just like you. You are the witness to that which you are: As yourself (when you self-reflect); your culture (when you celebrate and critique it); and this world (when you enjoy and protect it). When you grow and evolve, you heal yourself and the mistakes and traumas of a collective past.

You are the link between the past and the future, and therefore an agent of change. Every perception, insight, and truth *you have ever experienced* is nested in an unfolding grid that is timeless and boundless. The way you think, feel, and behave are all connected to the original impulse.

As the story goes…

From the original dust clouds of particles, to circulating, spiraling galaxies, the balance of matter and dark matter, and the imagination of basic elements, the creative force of the universe shines. With life emerging on Earth, rapid changes formed not only our planet but the whole cosmos. From the elemental bacteria that swam in the ancient waters of our planet to today's modern humans, life has been consistently updating its biological and psychological prototypes to have increased interaction with itself, from countless perspectives.

After the explosion of biological evolution, which started roughly four billion years ago, an inner supernova of consciousness emerged, and it radically changed the world we inhabit. Over the past 50,000 years, not much has changed in our physical appearance or genetic makeup, but we are almost unrecognizable from our ancestors. Think about it—in 15,000 years, a nanosecond in cosmic time, we moved from painting on cave-walls to doodling on iPads!

You were part of all of this—a 14.7 billion-year miracle in the making. You are literally made of stardust. You exist at a balance point between chaos and order, between being and becoming.

Equilibrium is your goal.
Evolution is your quest.

You are part of this wholeness that was, is, and always will be. You are, as Arthur Koestler (1967) put it, a "holon"[8]— something that is a whole and also a part of a much bigger story. You are a part of this whole that is your culture, the planet, and the universe. You are a whole and a part, and that means you matter more than you can ever imagine.

And maybe this part/whole that you are is why you don't fit. I mean, you probably function well, have a good job, and some good friends, but you don't fit in the given molds of how you *should* think and be. Maybe it is because you know in your bones that this force, that is in essence you, demands your attention to serve the impulse to evolve.

A force that is undefined.
Spontaneous and alive.
A dynamic intelligence.

Some people like to call it God. All infinite variations on
Him, Her, It, That, us, and you. And let's not get stuck on the
name, okay? Call it Spirit, Life, Essence, Source, Mystery,
Higher Power, the Cosmos, or anything that works for you.
For me, God is a verb: An emerging reality. Incomplete, but
whole. Still evolving, adapting, learning and growing. All
that we have ever loved, are loving or will love. All that we
have ever known as people, culture, and planet.

Present.
Perfect.
Progressive.

Instead of saying: *Everything that is, as space, at all times,
in all directions and dimensions, as evolution and in all stages
of development*, I say God. God is not *just* spirit or love or
the universe or anything that fits in such neatly defined
parameters, because God is alive and aliveness cannot be
contained or bounded.

God is not one thing.
Its expressions are endless.
It is the absence of God.
The world soul.

A non-dual suchness.
An ever-changing Cosmos.
It is all of these definitions, and more.
At once.

This is why, in Hebrew, God has many names representing different manifestations, why Hinduism includes a whole pantheon of gods to give voice to different aspects of creation, preservation, and destruction, and why Buddhists speak of *pointing at the moon*—the essential continuum that can never be described, but only gestured at.

No matter how deep you go, how profound your ideas may be, how awake you are, how expansive is your vision, it is only one of countless versions of reality. This realization is humbling and liberating because you are free to play, create, and engage with the many faces of God.

That is why I am in love with this idea of God. I love that my spiritual understanding might encompass a *fraction* of the infinite nature of God, that the only thing I know of this magical place I live in is my experience of divinity as it manifests in my body, thoughts, feelings, actions, and the relationships I have with others and with the natural world.

GENERATING REALITIES

Like so many people before me, I too want to bridge the gap of my experience toward a common ground of understanding and collaboration. I'm not interested in forming a common belief in God—I could not care less if we believe in the same imaginary God. I am also not seeking simply to arrive at a mutual respect for different ideas about God. Because, let's face it, people have done and are still doing some horrible things in the name of *God*.

Before we dive in any further, it is important to remember and name this. In every corner of the world, amoral leaders have corrupted religious and spiritual ideals and regular people have paid the price; through physical torture, cultural genocide, and abuse of power, religious leaders have suppressed basic human rights, and allowed atrocities to happen to people who they were supposed to shepherd. Religious zealots and fundamentalists destroy "evil" cultures and "sinful" neighbors in the name of their God/s.

I am sorry if this has happened to you, or your people and if you give me a chance, I hope I can explain why this keeps happening. And maybe, together, we can put an end to it by changing the way we *talk* and *think* about the story of God. I am seeking a common ground that is always new because it is alive and when God is alive and not just an idea (i.e., when we actively sense God between us), rigid conceptions and beliefs give way to curiosity, vulnerability, and love. I hope you want this as well.

Here's the thing. I believe that the impulse in the heart of the journey of God is two-fold: from *God to us* and from *us to God*. The former means that I can sense my oneness with all—the love, presence, and radical freedom that I hold. The latter means that through heeding the impulse to adapt, we help God know him/her/itself from all points of view.

Because the impulse keeps evolving.
And with it, God.

It always does — before life existed and within all cultures today. It changes with time, slowly shifting from its many premodern varieties to the modern search for rules that govern man and universe, and eventually to the pluralism of our time. Every single developmental stage, every idea, every perspective about self, life, and nature — is God changing. In all that change, in all that transformation and growth (and pain and horror), the impulse is always seeking a balance between stability and growth.

This is all for the sake of (and this is where things get a bit too mysterious, or woowoo, for some) love.[9] I don't believe you would have picked up this book if you didn't know this to be true in your heart. Despite the fact that you may not have a clear vision yet, you know that the current solutions on offer are, at best, limited and, at worst, toxic to our inner (and outer) ecologies.

This knowing is the impulse. It is the heart of your authentic, timeless, quest to know yourself. It is alive and endlessly creative. It never gets stuck. It is the indestructible quest to make meaning out of your life as a person and as a part of humanity — to provide answers and keep the thirst for a living manifestation of God. It is at the center of our cravings for physical and mental health, long-lasting joy, deeper connections, spiritual and psychological insight, artistic expression, inner peace, awe, and love. Jung (1963) writes:

> *The myth of the necessary incarnation of God...can be understood as man's creative confrontation with the opposites and their synthesis in the self, the wholeness of his personality...That is the goal...which fits man meaningfully into the schema of creation and at the same time confers meaning upon it (p.338).*

The (story of) God that Jung speaks of is not of a removed, masculine, all-knowing, ancient supernatural entity. Nor does it have an agenda. It is a love-manifestation that is so much more than any of us can imagine or feel. It is a love that only thrives in *form* and *time*. Each unique expression of (your) life is a whole world waiting to be known, asking to be understood in a distinct way. Every moment can be experienced as a treasure that is pregnant with the possibility of new breakthroughs.

> *You are a tiny pixel of love in an infinite creation.*
> *Limited only by your imagination.*

This love is not a one-sided longing for spiritual meaning, awakening to your true nature, or connection with the divine. It is a call for a relational *co-creative* engagement where you and I play critical roles. When we follow the impulse, our aliveness, we expand what is possible. We literally generate more *reality*.

We get to re-imagine our relationship to the primordial impulse that wants to know itself as life, nature, and the expanding universe. The impulse, as a collective force, is essential to a learning and growing God where you can choose to recreate the trinity of self, other (be in people or the natural world), and God. You also get to re-discover your responsibility not only for your own personal future, but also for the future of this planet.

This is *my* story of God, and in it I imagine that the longing is mutual. It is as if God were saying, "Help me to know myself." And through the power of that longing, love teaches me the language of life and the song of the cosmos.

I wish to support the spiritual misfits of the world in *reclaiming* their spiritual story. I want this not just for their own growth and peace of mind, but also for the sake of what is truly the greatest (or biggest) story ever told—the story of the mystery in which we live, and all of the infinite variations of *that*.

THE IMPULSE AS PRINCIPLES

As we follow the impulse, many can sense that we are on the brink of integrating cohesion and choice, self and other, belonging and freedom. But we won't be able to achieve this if we don't understand why we are divided and why so many walls of bigotry, fear, cynicism, apathy, and hate still separate us. Lately, these walls have been growing.

Sometimes it seems that the more you push, the more they close in on you. You attack, and the walls become thicker—as if resistance makes them stronger. A counterforce, more powerful than you, pushes back.

So many caring people I know are baffled by this. They can't get their heads around the fact that many *still* go against what seems to be common sense—people don't believe in climate change? Really? Islamophobia, antisemitism, and homophobia still exist in 2019? People are still killing in the name of particular God/s and religious beliefs?

I myself sometimes give in to defeat when I read the news or scroll through my social media feeds. What can I do to impact the world when the more I try, the more it seems to not make any difference? And the worst part is that these make-believe walls of separation have a real impact on people. They are the reason there is still so much hurt, hate, killing, torture, humiliation, and antagonism around the world. Those imaginary but restrictive walls prevent us from getting our act together on issues like climate change and other global predicaments.

If you follow the news, you will see passionate people from all sides of the political spectrum expressing frustration and upset. Each group believes that they have the moral and philosophical grounds to push their agenda, believes as if their way of life is being threatened by other groups. If you go just a bit deeper, you can start to see that, as Marshall Rosenberg, the founder of nonviolent communication, writes, they are all trying to meet their needs and be understood. The growing frustration and agitation can be seen as a request for empathy—to be heard and seen by members inhabiting different worldviews.

As with other human traits, empathy is a human attribute and a learned skill that needs to be cultivated culturally, *especially in non-homogenous societies*. And it is impossible to cultivate empathy without (usually unspoken) principles and social structures (such as schools, universities and so on) that provide dominant and minority groups with safety to express themselves. And here, for some, is the shocker: Empathy must include racist and fundamentalist groups because in many cases people who are thus labeled are not that at all.

By misinterpreting or mistranslating different worldviews, we miss learning about their subtleties and nuances. People are always more complex (beautiful, ugly, divine, mundane— you name it) than the labels we give them. This does not mean that you need to agree with people who offend you or have views that are at war with your core values; rather, it suggests that the focus of structural empathy should be on the *context of our time* and less on *the context of our ideas*. Life in the 21st century can feel *really* scary, complicated, and unstable.

This crisis of the mind haunts me. I know it demands a brave exploration of our current challenges, despite the personal discomfort this might cause. This impasse of worldviews requires a higher-tier vision that emerges from the original impulse—a *wider lens that can transform and interpret realities that appear to* be in conflict. Such a lens would be like a translator of source, an empathy tool, or a *(post)postmodern orientation* that includes earlier variations of the impulse. This orientation needs to be founded on the basic qualities of the impulse and, at the same time, it needs to be as inclusive and up to date with contemporary knowledge as possible.

Cultures and people evolve.
As should our cultural operating system.
And if humanity is to mirror the cosmic impulse,
No imitation of what has been done before will suffice.

When the call to write this book and share my message came, the patterns of the impulse were there to guide me toward this kind of orientation. I only had to segment them into elementary principles to make them as accessible to as many people as possible. I wanted to define patterns that manifested in as many worldviews and authentic spiritual traditions as possible. Patterns—not feel-good values, ideas, or beliefs. I wanted to avoid what I see as the over-simplification of religious values such as *the golden rule, heaven is within, love thy neighbor,* and *the now* to name just a few. I was looking for the patterns that form the basis of all formal religions, regardless of time, place, and culture.

From the beginning of life.
As we gathered and forged,
And created civilizations.
These patterns were in all traditions,
And day to day life.

I searched for the patterns that already unite people. The emerging cultural trajectory needs this. Evolving beyond limited perspectives means leaning into what has been there from the start—patterns that were so innate that people would understand them intuitively. I sought patterns that do not impose too much cultural content and values, but instead come from our biology, ecology and cosmology.

I wanted to find patterns that people can respect and understand, no matter what tradition they come from or what worldview they hold. I want communities to work with content that is relevant for them. I feel that if I provide content or build in my personal interpretation, I would undermine the creative potential and process of each community.

Finding patterns that connect was not easy or quick. I was searching for the most basic of forces to be used as principles in an open source algorithm of divinity. This took me a long time because I had to break down the traditions in many major religions of the world into their most basic elements. Eventually, foundational categories presented as principles.

I discovered that in each and every tradition there is always movement toward *complexification* and *diversification, balance* (or what can be referred as a dialectic tension between worldviews), alignment with the *rhythmic pulse* that is at the heart of every single moment, *creativity* as the basis for the chaotic and yet harmonic nature of the universe, and *acceptance* as the domain that engulfs all in a present perfect (but progressive) reality. The five organizing principles of the CODE were born from these patterns. Below are some simple descriptions of each of the principles:

Holism
THE GREAT WAY (ANTIDOTE TO ISOLATION)

System thinking, complexification, diversification, connection, time, evolution, adaptation, multi-directional movement.

We are all connected.
From the cell to the universe.
From the microbe to the planet as a whole.
All cherished. Sacred.
All limited and whole.

Our perceptions and actions are by their very nature limited, narrow, and restricted. Not wrong but constrained. They may be limited by their scale of validity, level of complexity, or capacity to hold diversity, among other reasons. No matter what you believe, how well researched your theory is, it is an incomplete yet important piece of the story.

The holonic perspective is critical for any community, especially those interested in bringing together the wisdom of the past with the needs of tomorrow. By having it as a guiding principle in your community, you will save so much time and effort! You won't have to fight over perspectives, or convince each other that you are right and others are wrong. Hallelujah! Instead, you will become curious about how *each* perspective has its place. What could have become a cause for fighting is thus transformed into a playful game of assembling a multi-layered and multi-directional puzzle.

This is why holonism is so unique—it does not disregard or discard knowledge or theories. Instead, it aims to integrate them into ever-expanding perspectives. New insights create new perspectives, making what once seemed complete, partial. All perspectives are validated and located in a chain of complexifying and diversifying cultural-social reality.

Rhythm
THE PULSE (ANTIDOTE TO HYPERVIGILANCE)

Spiral, circle, pulse, beat, coming and going, flow, in and out, breathing, seasons.

Aligning with nature, we breathe in.
Aligning with self, we breathe out.

Rhythm is a fundamental quality that can be found in the pulse of the expanding universe, nature, and the human body. The more you align with the basic rhythms of life, the more you feel balanced, present, and engaged. Indigenous cultures around the world knew this intuitively as they integrated rhythms into their ceremonies, holidays, and initiations to strengthen and maintain their alignment with their environment. Through spring equinox and winter solstice gatherings, harvest rituals, and seasonal ceremonies, ancient civilizations were dialed into a universal pulse.

The rhythmic pulse is a regulating force that helps you to pay closer attention to the means by which you find healthy patterns and a sustainable lifestyle. Without rhythms, societies tend to push too hard toward progress (or achievement). This *pursuit of more*, which in fact is an act of psychological avoidance, has caused millions of North Americans to engage in maladaptive patterns as a means to avoid suffering (myself included). As modern creatures, we have lost the natural, instinctual capacity to embrace the beat of our personal, cultural, and ecological rhythms. The more we became *civilized*, the more we fenced off parts of nature, and therefore began to lose track of the natural rhythmic pulse that once guided us.

As a principle of the CODE, the rhythmic pulse is there to remind you that any attempt to reform existing religions or bring about new religious models must have an awareness of the rhythmic circles that we all, always, rotate around. Being aligned, through practice, with the spiraling, turning, and returning nature of things will help you find a common beat with others. Each person will hold their own internal pulse, and each lineage will be guided by it's unique beat. Through attention to and integration of these rhythms, our inner lives and outer circumstances *can* find a common ground so equilibrium may be (re)established.

Creativity
WHEN EVERYTHING GOES (ANTIDOTE FOR FEAR)

Multiplicity, trust, illusions, imagination, choice, willingness, freedom, discernment, intent.

Creativity is a deep longing for stability. The universe and life as we know it are in a constantly chaotic and yet somehow harmonious dance. Ceaselessly fruitful, it is like a wish-fulfilling gem. This creativity is the birthplace of art, philosophy, and science. It also produced the powerful devices of destruction, hateful belief systems, and suffering.

You are the spontaneity and creativity of life that is movement and change. You are never the same. As Heraclitus, a Greek philosopher born circa 544 BCE, wrote, "You cannot step twice into the same river." This inability to hold onto anything (and therefore cement meaning) is a key element in the process of maturation as a person and in culture. Life spills into death (or endings), and from death, a fresh moment arises. You then learn that you do not have the ability, in reality, to hold on and therefore are free to be the dynamic self that you already are.

As a principle of the CODE, creativity is your permission to imagine. It prompts you to say yes to the creative force that comes through you. Instead of forcing a set of laws and rules on the dynamic energy of God, or believing that our version of reality is (truly) real, this principle guides you to hold the tension of vulnerability in creativity, while always also letting go.

Presence
TAPPING INTO WHAT IS ALREADY PERFECT
(ANTIDOTE FOR SUFFERING)

Wholeness, ease, the nature of the mind, insight, the field of reality.

Duality means that there are two sides to every story. Yin and yang. Push and pull. The stuff that makes up your psychological existence. It is the water in which you swim — so much so that we do not recognize that we constantly divide almost each and every moment, experience, and interaction. In fact, life is interdependent and interconnected. Like images appearing in a mirror or waves in the ocean, the non-dual reality field is the ultimate state of consciousness. It remains unaffected by anything, and yet is everything. With no beginning or end and without limitation, it can be likened to the open sky, which is never affected by the clouds. You have the innate capacity to know yourself as this. I am not exaggerating. This presence is not a supernatural or special state. Rather, it is a deepening of your embodied human experience. It is your ticket to a fearlessly examined life, where you can relax into what is, where you don't need to be anybody, do anything, or go anywhere.

Balance

YES, NO AND MAYBE...? (ANTIDOTE TO RIGIDITY)

'Both and...', win win win scenarios, dialectics.

From the beginning of time, balance brought the fundamental forces in the universe together to create giant dust clouds that produced stars, planets, and eventually life. Without it, the universe as we know it would have collapsed long ago into singularity or drifted apart so intensely that all we would see, or be, is isolated atoms across the vastness of time and space.

The principle of balance reminds us that all forces — physiological, biological or psychological — are meant to work together despite their inherent tension. Reality is a balancing act among all of the forces that make our universe and our civilizations tick.

In the CODE, balance is understood as a dynamic energy that evolves with time, adapting to new circumstances and external complexities. It is the creative tension that leads to a synergy, where two opposing worldviews are resolved or held together as a new, more alive, complex, and agile worldview.

Cℜ

These five principles, in my view, are some of the most universal and basic principles that I have found in my research. They are foundational to any collaborative work and they are simple (enough… I hope). The main point is to see that they exist in all worldviews and as such can be a bridge for better communication and collaboration. I will say much more about them in Part two. For now, I will only add that I am not going to assume that they are the right ones for you and your community. If you need to add or change them, go ahead. I am sure that with time, and as this book is debated and criticized, there will be many adaptations of and additions to the principles.

The principles are not only intended to function as techniques for creating a collaborative spirituality. They are also intended to help your process come alive, because they prevent groups from landing on any one perspective, or from becoming content with simple answers. The quality of mind they evoke is radical because they are already present in all our collective stories, and yet they point to the freedom to re-invent ourselves..

Humanity has mastered the right conditions for civilizations to emerge, for science to advance, and for the self to individuate. Now, our next tasks is to learn how to better integrate and collaborate across worldviews, political affiliations, and cultures.

We need answers to questions we don't even know that we are asking.

Our old stories can become the compost that nurtures the questions of *this* time. Like a seed waiting for rain and sunshine, they will flourish once again, and bear fruit. Then we will find out that everything can be holy, even death. The conditions are ripe to discover these questions and once these questions sprout, you will begin to notice transformation. You will become more yourself.

As self,
As relationships,
As science,
As *God*.

RELIGIOUS
CONTEXT

Where I explain why religions are only boxes
that need to be expanded, not discarded.

3 | INFINITY IN A BOX

*Religion: "Gathering all energy on all levels,
to bring about attention and in that attention
there is movement. Gathering of total energy
to understand what thought cannot possibly
capture. Thought is never new, never free and
therefore fragmented." –J. Krishnamurti*

God and religion. Talk about loaded terms! What do these words mean to you? What feelings do they conjure? How do they connect to you being a spiritual misfit? Notice any positive or negative associations you may have with them. Notice how your personal context, cultural-historical background, family heritage and lineage, spiritual-religious experience, all affect your relationship with these words.

> *Even if you don't believe in God,
> if you don't belong to any tradition,
> You have been influenced.*

Over ten thousand (or so) years of religious development, our understanding of God and its place in our lives evolved. The friction between worldviews has defined your current perception of the role that God and religion plays in your life and how you understand their value to yourself and to society (for better and for worse).

This unbroken continuum of religious evolution is the reason you, as a spiritual misfit, matter. You have the capacity to understand that continuum and the part you need to play in shaping the next iteration of this evolving essence. While some may oppose *or* embrace religion, others do not even think about it. But *you* can sense the significance of holding both positions, because you see the need to help religion (as a general notion, not any specific religion) to change once again. Because *religion*, as an oppressive structure, and *God*, as a premodern idea, are still *very* present in our politics, social norms, and ethics around the world. They affect the life of people. They suppress choice and oppress minorities. And if we don't do more to make our stories more encompassing and to build new ones, the *old gods* that are out of touch with our present needs will continue to dominate our psyche and, to some degree, our societies.

And because consciousness can shrink back to older, more familiar worldviews, progressive and liberal countries are always, and still, at risk of being exposed to this kind of religious influence.

Humans (and the natural world) have suffered horrifically because of premodern religious ideologies. Try to think about religion, any religion, without cruelty, hate, greed, or pain. Not easy, right? This, sadly, does not exclude any of the major religions of the world and is still a painful reality for many. Our history is full of men and women (let's face it, mostly men) who used religion to control others by seeking power and financial gain. "Holy wars" have been fought on every continent in the world — inquisitions, pogroms, tribal warfare. There are literally thousands of books on how religious people have killed, raped, burned, tortured, and imprisoned others "in the name" of one or another God or gods. Nations, endlessly manipulated by politicians and religious leaders, enslaved and brutalized other humans.

I empathize with those who wish for a world without religion and God. I understand the allergy people have to the word *religion* and what it represents. For many, the word summons notions of oppression, abuse of power, greed, and violence. Many believe that, once and for all, it is time to throw the baby out with the bathwater.

Why try to work with a broken system?
A false idea?
Why should we re-imagine religion?
Why not, as John Lennon famously sang, *imagine no religion?*

The short answer is that religion is not going anywhere soon. In some parts of the world, the opposite is happening—premodern religious models are growing! According the Pew Research Center, more than 80% of the world population is still religious. I will come back to this number, but for now let me just say that religion cannot cease to be, because it is not only a structure, but also a longing for self-knowledge *in the public domain* that has always sought novel expressions. Always. And as such, it can only change. Not end.

RELIGION IS AN EVOLVING CONCEPT

Your personal spiritual journey is key to your happiness, but it is not enough if you care for others and this world. If you cannot go back to a tradition (or choose only one tradition), and yet feel unsettled by your spiritual isolation, then you have tapped into the significant role you play in the unfolding of an emerging new consciousness that is much bigger than just the role spirituality plays in your life. This is why context is so important—a context that is wider and bigger than your personal spiritual story of healing and awakening.

If we strip religion, any religion, to its essence, we will find that it is but a social construct that assists with making sense of the world. It functions to support spiritual and psychological growth on a *collaborative*, interpersonal level.

This is what religion does so well that individual spirituality does not. It binds people together, for mutual emergence, regardless of the content of any specific religion. That same essence moves through us *now* seeking new, more collaborative, and complex formations. And the carriers are those who do not fit already established religious forms but who still want to take part in collaborative spirituality.

In the end, religion is nothing but a box that holds a smidgeon of infinity. And when I write 'smidgeon', I mean just that. To say it differently, religion has always been an attempt to put infinity in a box (good luck!) and that is why it is so seductive, effective, and when unchecked, dangerous.

Each box creates a wholly distinctive experience for people and cultures. On a fundamental level, all of these boxes run on the same impulse. However, each and every box is different on multiple levels — from the individual level through micro structures like families and communities, all the way up to the macro-structures of societies. All define what kind of psychological and cultural applications a person can and can't run.

| *We are both the creators of our realities and a creation of our box.* |

Humans have a *built in need* to make these boxes. We have always done this. Some of us replace premodern religious boxes with modern ones (like humanism) and postmodern ones (like relativism and pluralism), but impulse to make boxes remains constant.

When we start to think about religious boxes in this way, we can get curious and see that religious structures have morphed over time and that we can participate in continuing to evolve them without attacking other boxes. This approach involves more than just including other people's religious boxes (i.e., showing tolerance). It is, rather, a way of occupying many boxes at once.

We can create *dynamic* and *evolving* boxes that work for our complex times, where all formations—past and present—have value.

Some will say that their box is the *only* box or that the box they believe in is *better* than yours; that if you don't use their box you will *never* understand God or be religious. Let them. I am going to show you why they might be (partly) right, how to work with people who think this way, and how to work with them to make wider, more inclusive, and more resilient boxes.

Because, let me tell you,
You are stuck in a box.
We all are.

Resisting religion?
You are stuck in a box!

Believe in God?
You are stuck in a box…

Love what I am saying?
You are stuck in a box.

There is no "no box."

Just the possibility of widening the box.

Our mind is endlessly creative, but it also tends to fall in love with its own creation, tricking itself into believing that its creation is real. This, in turn, make us believe that our worldview has independent substance, when in fact it is a psycho-cultural structure that adapts with time. In other words, people usually wind up worshipping the structure (the box) instead of the mystery that cannot be fully explained.

Mental and physical phenomena exist in relation to our perceptions and conceptions, not because they are real. We need those structures to function but can also hold them lightly, knowing that they are part of the mind's imagination, and therefore of God—always creative, always harmonious. Each and every worldview (box) on the spiral of consciousness is a stepping stone, a dialectical tension that can be challenged and adapted constantly. From a deep-time perspective, this is what religion has done for centuries. By its very essence, religion as a box is adaptable and developmental. It is when we put our story of what religion is into inflexible categories that we miss its infinite playfulness.

We tend to confuse infinity with the box, when in fact it is *always* the boxes that create suffering. It is the worldview that defines one's religious orientation (or tendencies), not the other way around. In other words, it is the box and not infinity that determines what any given religion or spiritual path looks and functions like. This may sound obvious to you, but for a premodern religious person, this idea might make little sense. How can we work with, embracing their point of view while also seeing beyond it?

To bring people together in a more collaborative and harmonious way, we need to build bridges that are creative and mindful of where each person is really at. A solid bridge takes time to build. The bridges of tomorrow will not be built on theory, dogma, or moralistic doctrines, but in the orientation to what is available (already) in *all* boxes.

Boxes (can) change.
Thank God for that.

God and religion *are* loaded terms, I know. But they are here to stay. So, I invite you to be open and curious about the religious structures that can help religion mature. Spirituality, science, psychology, and other elements of human existence can come together after being fragmented for the past millennia, and with that, we will embrace what was always suppose to (eventually!) happen— The dawn of integration.

LIFE AFTER DIVORCE:
FROM PRE- TO POST-RELIGION

In the past, our spiritual needs were met in ways that are profoundly different from today, but the longing remains consistent. In ages past, people were mostly born, raised, and died in cultures that embraced one particular religion. This is certainly not the case for most of us now. In today's spiritual marketplace, our need for meaning, connection, love, significance, and belonging can be met in so many ways. One can opt to join an already existing religion or spiritual organization, or they might cherry pick aspects from a variety of traditions to form a unique, individualized path.

For the first time in history, we have almost infinite and immediate access to historical knowledge, to almost any idea, from any era, from around the world. We are now almost unrestricted in what we can learn, know, and believe. If you live in a somewhat progressive society, you can choose how and if you worship. You can choose what kind of story you want to tell about the universe. You get to choose and create your own spiritual maps.

The breakdown of big truths into fragmented perspectives has allowed for freedom of thought and action. There is greater respect for diversity and identity, and acceptance of the individual journey. However, there is not as much genuine collaboration between worldviews. It is still rare to see ideological, spiritual, intellectual, and psychological gaps being bridged. Fostering mutual respect and valuing diversity might be the building blocks of a tolerant society, but they do not necessarily support integration.

It is true that we don't need religion in science, academic research, governance, or in schools. We don't even need religion in our day to day lives. Many have chosen to put religion aside, either describing themselves as spiritual, agnostic, or atheist. In simple terms, premodern religions have given way to scientific inquiry, humanistic ideals, and postmodern relativism (and fragmentation). After being enmeshed for thousands of years in structures that did not serve anymore, people revolted and stories changed. We were not the children of God, but rather independent adults figuring it out on our own.

One might think of it as a long-term marriage that went sour—for centuries most of humanity was *in a relationship* with one version or another of religion. Often, those religious structures took advantage of or even abused people. But, with time and growing awareness (collectively, as consciousness) many decided to end that marriage. It wasn't working any longer. As a result of healthier boundaries and a clearer understanding of human potential, we entered a new chapter. We divorced religion.

Finally, we had the freedom to be the masters of our own destiny, and thus the age of the *absent God* emerged. As we shattered our ties to the old God/s and developed reverence for science and (hyper?) individualism in the West, we broke free from the bondage of our religious past. Human worship was focused on things, ideas, and people instead of God/s.[10]

Ultimately, what was pushed away came back in the form of unrealistic demands from our new teachers, lovers, therapists, and politicians, and expectations to create heaven on earth through science and political movements (Hillman, 1975).

I want you to really *hang out* with this notion for a moment: As modern people, many have transmuted the need for religion and sublimated its original meaning. The eternal symbolic power of religion has morphed into relational, political, and secular aims and values. New boxes were created.

We all know that there is a lot of bad blood between science and religion. Some want to hijack science to explain their religious views, while others use science to debunk religious ideas. They don't see any need for a God, be it a static or an evolving God. They believe that this backward notion of God in a world that can be explained by science is not only irrelevant, but dangerous. According to this view, spiritually is a personal choice, and should stay in the private as opposed to public domain.

I believe that what most atheists are doing is rejecting premodern or modern versions of God, and not the interpretation of God that is proposed in this book. They are rejecting older variations (not bad, or primitive, just earlier versions) of god as an idea. For example, Dr. Richard Dawkins tends to mock religions for promoting a "spaghetti monster in the sky," and he argues that religious people base their faith solely on belief in a "non-existent," supernatural entity. He emphasizes the need for logical conclusions and evidence that can be perceived with the senses, and puts no stock in *belief*. Now, to some extent Dr. Dawkins is right. It is impossible to prove the existence of God, and in my opinion, it would be also pointless.[11]

I see the beauty and validity in all authentic spiritual traditions. I also value atheist movements as I believe they represent a critical developmental step in the maturation of God. I am guessing that for some atheists, this sounds absurd, and I understand why! The journey of God to know itself is not one-dimensional. It is a developmental and creative process. Proclaiming that the essence of religion only belongs to what we call organized religions is to miss the rhythm of the co-creative dance. The *impulse* was present before the emergence of the great traditions and will continue after they dissolve. The evolution of culture from premodern to more humanistic structures is yet another version of the same impulse. This means that atheism can be perceived as one more manifestation of divinity. As Martin Buber (1937) proposed:

> *He who knows the world as something by which he is to profit knows God also in the same way. His prayer is a procedure of exoneration heard by the ear of the void. He—not the 'atheist,' who addresses the Nameless out of the night and yearning of his garret-window—is the godless man"* (p. 107).

The story of God is always defined by the knowledge of an era, because God is as dynamic as the cultures that *imagine him*. So, how we relate to God morphs with time. We have worshiped countless gods and then killed God. We replaced it with science, political ideologies, and even celebrity worship. We have moved from a moralistic, dogmatic spirituality to an individualistic search for meaning.

In other words, the map (our consciousness, through emerging insights) expands the territory of God. Something keeps being made out of nothing. The mind of God is thus not unlike the universe, which constantly expands into nothingness.

| *Love literally grows through our thoughts, and actions.* |

And with that grows choice and responsibly for ourselves, others, and nature as players in the evolution of God.

From this deep time perspective, you start to realize the value of each and every worldview that has emerged through history and why it is critical not only to respect them but also to integrate them into our ever-expanding maps of consciousness. No variation of the story of the universe is ever complete.

I don't believe we can afford to collapse all this juiciness into only one perspective — be it inclusive, modern, diverse, or scientific. The impulse will always push for more integration (of past and present) and complexification for its own growing awareness and self-actualization. And, most importantly, it is striving for a future that does not look like any variation we are currently familiar with. The structures of tomorrow will allow the impulse to thrive, so we can serve the greatest aspect of who we are *as* that impulse.

To paraphrase the great American philosopher and religious scholar Jacob Needleman, we are at the cusp of bridging the gap between modern science and ancient spiritual worldviews. This is seen in the eruption of numerous new religions, most of which find their sources in the religions of the Eastern world. Needleman points to the heart of what many of us trust is the real story here — the attempts to integrate heart and mind, past and present, diversity and mastery.

> *We are searching for an updated roadmap to bridge what we feel and what we know.*

This task is daunting and yet exciting because it presents an opportunity to integrate the great treasures of authentic spiritual traditions with contemporary knowledge.

Many people do not see any value in premodern religions. I can understand that. But this does not mean that we cannot develop a new kind of relationship with the divine.[12] The original need that drove us to ask questions to better know our place and to know ourselves will never stop, with or without religion. It is funny to write a book about religion and the evolution of God while harboring a gut intuition that, at the end of the day, the next evolutionary step of God might not include God as an idea — that, God, as the essence of all that was, is, and will be, might just have to hide behind the cultural curtains of our times.

GOD UNDER CONSTRUCTION

Humans have a fundamental *need* for authentic spiritual structures, which in simple terms is a need for *synchronization*. Whether we are conscious of it or not, we are all pulled to synchronize self, other, the natural world, with the great mysteries. It is *impossible* to avoid or suppress this need without a strong backlash. According to Dr. Stephen Porges, the founder of the polyvagal theory, the backlash can manifest as too much energy (busyness, anxiety, being overwhelmed, overconsumption, addiction) or a general feeling of being shut down, depleted, disoriented, depressed, or disengaged.[13]

Now, as we know, a need is something that is required because it is very important. It is a *necessity*. If you follow this definition, when do spiritual structures become *necessary*?

I am going to make the case that the *essence* of religion, as opposed to the word and its historical baggage, is a necessity. As mentioned before, more than eighty percent of the world's population is still religious. That is a significant number of people who will play a part in future economic and political constructions, and how we, as a global community, might deal with issues such as looming ecological crisis, global warming and rising geopolitical tension.

Religion is here to stay due to cultural, historical, anthropological, economic, and psychological factors. For now, let's just review some of the statistics. If current trends continue, by 2050:

ક Atheists, agnostics, and other people who do not affiliate with any religion will make up a *declining* share of the world's total population.

ક The global Buddhist population will be about the same size it was in 2010, while the Hindu and Jewish populations will be larger than they are today.

ક In the United States, Christians will decline from more than three-quarters of the population in 2010 to two-thirds in 2050, and Judaism will no longer be the largest non-Christian religion. Muslims will be more numerous in the United States than people who identify as Jewish on the basis of religion.

ક The number of Muslims will nearly equal the number of Christians around the world.

ક In Europe, Muslims will make up 10% of the overall population.

ક India will retain a Hindu majority but also will have the largest Muslim population of any country in the world, surpassing Indonesia.

ક Four out of every ten Christians in the world will live in sub-Saharan Africa.[14]

As you can see, all indications are that religion will remain a powerful, growing force around the world for many years. Getting rid of what the religious heart provides to the human spirit is not only dangerous, but impossible on a *collective level*. For those who choose to look the other way, make fun of religious people, or believe that we can get rid of the space it occupies in our psyche, I say—religion is here to stay. *So, instead of denying and rejecting it, I propose that instead we focus on dialoguing and adapting.* This, in my view, is essential because:

> *When we don't offer a future, people will choose a*
> *familiar past.*
> *But when we forget our past, we have no future —*
> *And what is left is a past that keeps repeating itself.*
> *Again, and again, and again.*
>
> *So here is a question for you:*
> *What parts of religion do we want running the show?*

We either integrate its essential parts, or the less life-giving aspects will continue to dominate our politics, culture, and society. This is the point that many miss. The elemental impulse behind all religions will continue to lead people to one or more forms of religion—if not a religious or spiritual tradition, then celebrity worship, political cults, an ideology, or the worship of power and money. When we ignore this timeless impulse, *this need*, we miss the fullness of our collective human experience and in some cases loose balance.

Our *existential* problems have dramatically shifted over the past forty years. As a result of increasing complexity and diversity in our socio-cultural structures, there has been a swing back to less inclusive worldviews—not bad or wrong, just less inclusive. The tension resulting from the expectation that one should be able to exhibit a profound flexibility and dynamism in values, beliefs, and ideals has become overwhelming for many and produce a backlash reaction.

Growing diversity yields countless perspectives on what reality is, and this can be disorienting, even terrifying, for that part of us that needs certainty and clarity. When things start to move and change too quickly, a flexible embrace of newly emergent, diverse cultural forms may be abandoned in favor of what is known, secure and clear—the answers of the past. This kind of regression to familiar roadmaps, as seen in fundamentalist forms of religiosity, is on the rise, and will continue to rise.

Safety will always trump change when there is not enough stability in the system.

Complexity produces anxiety which in turn produces efforts to bring back order. The pendulum swings back. That is why democratic countries are in greater danger than ever before of being taken over by authoritarian leaders, and why we are witnessing declining tolerance towards diversity in multicultural societies. All of this can be taken as evidence of the current ambiguity of consciousness. The scope and magnitude of what we are currently dealing with is unprecedented. We are in the midst of a giant global *wake up call* to adapt. [15]

To be clear, I'm not advocating for a religious life. I'm suggesting that we either integrate the religious *elements* that sustain and nourish us, or we get to deal with the unconscious aftermath of cutting significant developmental aspect of our collective existence.[16]

The painful truth is that when human beings are not nurtured or lack opportunities to meet their deepest needs for social inclusion and a sense of belonging and meaning, they will respond in one (or sometimes both) of two ways:

First, they will get the need met in any way possible, regardless of how feasible or maladaptive that solution is. This may include joining a gang, cult, or any other power-driven group, usually but not always with extreme or simplified points of view. Secondly, the person will develop strategies to avoid emotional pain and to block discomfort in themselves. Examples include nihilism, materialism, emotional numbness, and any form of avoidance (e.g., by indulging in porn, alcohol, substances, shopping, online usage, gambling, and so on).

Our core need to find boxes will never go away. My concern is that the lack of much needed *updated* and *relevant* religious structures (in the *widest* sense of that word) is resulting in the rise of four major social (and maladaptive) patterns:

Regression to fundamentalist beliefs, be it through established religious models, spiritual cults, or extreme views from the left and right of the political map. This radicalization combined with low empathy on both sides is fragmenting an already destabilized system. Regression into extreme perspectives is a response to a world that is changing too rapidly and an attempt to seek equilibrium in an ever more complex world. Rollo May (1989), the influential American existential psychologist, speaks to the reason people are willing to give away their freedom and power in face of too much change:

> *The ultimate error is the refusal to look evil in the face. This approach of evil—and freedom along with it—is the most destructive approach of all. To take refuge with... any cult... is to find haven where our choices will be made for us. We surrender freedom because of our inability to tolerate moral ambiguity, and we escape the threat that one might make the wrong choice. (p. 277)*

The rise of ethnocentric belief systems is causing the re-emergence of bigotry, prejudice, and xenophobia. It is important to make a distinction here between healthy ethnocentric qualities (e.g., family values, cultural homogamy, and so on) and the side effect of ethnocentric belief systems (us versus them). It is not surprising that in today's political climate, facts matter less than beliefs, and that humanitarian values are hitting up against apathy to the struggles of anyone who is not part of *my tribe*. These kinds of extremes are rampant in global politics, academic settings, and religious rhetoric. Inflammatory rhetoric is building momentum, and basic human rights are flailing:

A kind of a **cultural dead-zone** that according to research leads many to a life of heightened anxiety, isolation, depression and addictions and deprivation from cultural and spiritual meaning. In this view, addictions of any kind can be seen as an act of despair and an unconscious attempt to hold on to what was once alive and now is (spiritually) deemed dead. If an individual cannot feel safe enough or capable of processing his or her confusion and grief over being exiled from an original cultural home and from psychologically supportive environments, at least he or she may act out in maladaptive behaviors that serve as coping skills. Alexandra Cook (2012) (and others) reflect on this growing phenomenon:

Exposure to chronic, prolonged traumatic experiences such as social isolation and dislocation have the potential to alter people's brains (especially children's brains), which may have long-term effects on attachment, physical health, emotional regulation, and behavioral control (para 2). [17]

The rise of **superficial and hyper-individualistic** lifestyles, or what Jean Twenge and Keith Campbell refer to as the "the epidemic of narcissism." And Ken Wilber (2018) brilliantly adds: "Since everything handed to us by yesterday is not a real and enduring truth, just a fabricated fashion of history, it is our job to accept none of it, and instead only strive for a total, self-created, self-initiated autonomy...which very soon became indistinguishable from 'Nobody interferes with my narcissism!'" (p. 5).

The rise of these reactions scares me. They are a real concern. What we are seeing at the fringe of popular culture is a horizontal counterculture of psychological contraction. All four of these patterns can be seen as adaptive responses to a culture that is unable to adjust to the growing complexities of our times. Attack them and they will grow. Constantly become offended and watch how these fear-based reactions transform into hate.

And if you think I am being overly dramatic, notice the counter-response around the world to values of pluralism, multiculturalism, diversity, and freedom of thought. Notice who is winning elections. Follow the bloggers, the writers, and (if you really want too, though I would not recommend it), YouTube commenters.

These four reactions are a reminder that resistance, ridicule, and exerting a sense of superiority toward worldviews that one does not agree with do not work. People do not change when they feel shamed and pressured. People change when they are *ready* to change. In fact, the more we push people to think and act in ways that align with our own thinking, the more we will witness pushback and reactive outcomes that we did not intend and do not want.

The new frontier of the collective mind is not an end, but a movement that *ebbs and flows* from the past to the present, slowly touching the future— our collective journey is not linear in its pattern of growth. Each time a person or a culture evolves, what originally seemed impossible becomes plausible—consider, for example, gay marriage, women's rights, and so on. As people and cultures evolve, their worldviews stretch to include more of reality. But when the dominant worldview is too rigid (or too progressive), people tend to contract.

The four adaptations outlined above will continue to grow if we don't offer solutions that speak to each and every personal and collective developmental need, in correlation with the current emergence of the impulse.

Now zoom out. Think millions of people. People who do not feel that their voices matter, that their fears are recognized, and that their perspectives are respected.

Maybe you are one of those people? When you hear a new idea for the first time, you initially feel fear, danger, or insecurity. You want to keep an open mind and ask questions, but you don't feel invited to participate and you fear that you will be judged if you share your views, questions, and concerns.

Surprised by the statistics I shared about religion growing?
Wondering why we see a surge in authoritarian leadership?
Or why we are experiencing a swing back
towards ethnocentrism?
Don't understand how is it that people still choose
to believe in premodern versions of God?

These phenomena will continue to grow until we reclaim a *wider story of God* and enter an age of integration. This is because the co-creative dance with God is a *need*. If it is not made conscious and relevant, there will be dire consequences for our world. A commitment to human progress requires a willingness to genuinely learn from the past, explore the span of knowledge we currently hold, and heal old wounds, together.

Unless we can integrate these collective traumas and surmount our defenses, the cycle of pain and harm will continue. We cannot justify hurting people, communities, and our earth because of a religious or anti-religious agenda. When we do, the opposite of our intended result is created.

Adaptation (which is part of our capacity to evolve) goes beyond programs, tools, and theory. It is an embodied shift in the way we understand and live our life on a relational level, be it to others, the natural world and the divine forces that guide us.

This happens not only on a personal level, which is where we usually focus our attention, but also in the relational and cultural domain, in the ways we communicate and interact with one another. So, danger brings with it opportunities and, to those who listen, it also awakens a radical presence. In the intermediate state of change, humankind is still wandering between two worlds—one dying, the other powerless to be born. [18]

We are shifting.

We have been the children of God for millennia.
Then were left alone in the universe, as orphans.
We were asked to grow up.

To believe in our humanity,
But the ills of choice,
Brought us to question
The loss of our depth,
And the loneliness of our freedom.
What new form will you choose with others?

4 | RECLAMING GOD

You possess the rarest of
elements — a most precious gem.
Never again will God see through our
eyes. I invite you to come to terms
with this truth and live accordingly.

As we have seen, the great spiritual and psychological traditions are expressions of the divine impulse. This is true also of the developmental journey of all civilizations, including modern, secular ones. Nothing escapes this playful and creative force. This does not mean that all religions point in the same direction, or that they are all pathways to the same end. Holding such a point of view minimizes the specificity and uniqueness of each tradition and flattens the always-evolving and diversifying nature of consciousness.

I am saddened that in today's world, people tend to equate religion with institutionalized forms of religion rather than with what so many of us feel in moments of deep connection to ourselves, others, nature, and the universe. Being religious does not mean that you have to choose to belong to an organized religion or attend religious gatherings in a church, mosque, temple, or synagogue. Religion is about *intent* — to serve life on earth, while reality (of what I like to call *God*) learns and grows through and with you.

To be clear, you do not have to believe in heaven, hell, karma, souls, or any other spiritual concept to be religious! You do not even have to believe in God or gods. This is because the call of the spiritual misfit is to life as a creative inquiry. And this is what moves you.

This impulse can be experienced as the love you feel when you pray or meditate, in the I-Thou moments you share with others and nature, and in the passion and purpose of your life. It can also be experienced in what usually we do not attribute to a religious life, like in humanism, science, individualism, pluralism, and atheism.

It is *all* the dance.
It is *all* God.

So, what is the appeal of *reclaiming* God and religion in an era of personal spirituality and cultural fragmentation? For the spiritual misfit, it is a choice to stay in the ring of social change, to transcend the personal aspects of spiritual growth to include *dialogue* and collaboration with others, to choose not to be just a bystander in the evolution of the collectives.

While I was writing this book, friends often asked me why I chose to write about religion. "It's so old school!" they would say. "Call it, 'advanced spirituality' or make this a self-help model." I agreed, but in the end could not deny an impulse to write about religion and God. Despite the fact that for many God is not an *in* word, and religion is definitely not sexy or trendy, I made a choice to reclaim them.[19] I maintain that spirituality is a word that belongs to the personal domain. It is a safe, friendly word. It is hard to fight over it because it is so private.

Through my travels and research, I have come to the conclusion that most modern seekers are on a personal, psycho-spiritual journey. Rarely do you see collaborative spiritual work that resembles what religious structures can provide. Although personal work is necessary for the development of a healthy human psyche, it is not enough on its own. From a deep-time perspective, individuation and maturation should be viewed as both a standalone developmental achievement *and* as a stepping stone along the journey of the small self coming to know it's (very limited) place in the world.

It seems to me that many modern spiritual people are truly fearful of what religion has come to represent in their minds. They are legitimately cautious of anything that even remotely resembles religion. They worry that embracing religion could jeopardize their ability to think critically and make independent choices—all the *good stuff* that was achieved in secular societies. To some extent, these are reasonable concerns.

Freedom of thought, critical thinking, scientific research, and human rights emerged with the advent of humanism and the disavowal of the great traditions in the West. But along with this shift, many also lost touch with the potential of the story of *us*. The focus shifted, making *me* the main character of the story, while the religious *us* gave way to other types of utilitarian *us*.

The civil *us*
The country of *us*
The group identity *us*.
The multicultural *us*.

I use "utilitarian" because the focus of these social collectives is to serve the individual and protect their rights. The religious *us*, by contrast, was focused primarily on serving God (or the impulse "God" represents), not *only* humankind. By attempting to split religion from the state, we assumed a sense of freedom from the premodern dogma. By doing so, we accidentally 'split' God, leaving premodern versions of religion in a state of arrested development. Permitted to influence people only in the private domain, premodern religions lingered in the shadows of modern society.

I have tried repeatedly to find a word to replace "religion" that would still describe the essence of what I am trying to convey, but I have not found it. The best I have found was inspired by Pierre Teilhard de Chardin (1965), a French philosopher and Jesuit priest, that writes:

For a reflective being, such an eagerness for self-fulfillment can fundamentally be found only in the expectation of a supreme Summit of consciousness, which can be attained, and so provide a permanent home. And such a hope inspired faith in some future consummation cannot, in turn, take any form but that of a 'religion' in the truest, and most psychologically apt, meaning of the word (p. 26).

I too am aiming to use religion in the "truest, and most psychologically apt, meaning of the word." It is the reason I wrote this book. I am writing about religion as a felt, though unseen force, that grates against your resistance so that you can face the mystery of life—something that is bigger than you, and that you are in an intimate relationship with.

Religion cannot be frozen in time. Despite the persistence of premodern versions of religion and their profound resistance to change, religious structures did transform through the centuries. We can track changes in all of the great spiritual traditions and doing so helps us to see that each iteration grows out of earlier ones, like a city that is built on ruins.

Religious structures must change with the shifting realities of each era. Now, it is our time and responsibility as spiritual misfits to play our part in this story. What makes our task so unique is that for the first time in human history we are leaping from a focus on individual journeys and resulting fragmentation toward a focus on collaboration and integration.

You do not need to let go of or change who you are in order to develop an awakened and respectful relationship with others and the divine. Most importantly, *you* are needed to make it happen because it is only those who can comfortably inhabit multiple perspectives that have the capacity to reclaim religion.

THE FUTURE OF GOD

I know that it is possible to develop and implement religious models that can represent and include expanding worldviews, including psychological, humanistic, and even atheistic perspectives. I also recognize that with the right kind of process, people *can* have diverse and opposing worldviews, and still collaborate in a meaningful way.

How do I know all this? I lean on my personal experience as a group facilitator, but also on the work of Ken Wilber who has dedicated his life to mapping consciousness. Wilber's integral theory has inspired hundreds of thousands of people. His work has paved the way for many to imagine a future where developmental, psychological, cultural, and spiritual processes can coexist in communities. His work takes you to the edge of our collective known inner universe.[20]

I want to understand what happens when people actually arrive at that edge as members of a community.

To be clear, my curiosity about post individual spiritual work is not a throwback to spiritual enmeshment, and I am not referring to traditional religious structures. Yes, the new story is one of collectives, but it also values and fully embraces the personal journey towards individuation. The integration of personal spirituality and co-creative work is essentially a marriage of *diversity* and *hierarchy*.

Nothing that we have already tried will do.
The ingredients may be the same,
but what is cooking is fresh from the universal oven.

The future of God is the potential integration of all that has been discovered and accomplished to allow God to know itself from the countless layers and perspectives of existence. *Integrating the past* and *moving beyond focus on the individual* are key ingredients in the next step of spiritual work. To me, the questions remains open: Is there a path beyond individual spirituality that does not include a regression into tribal or ethnocentric mindsets? Can there be a group identity that does not consume individuals? These questions are not merely philosophical. They come straight from the *source*.

God has no future without us carving it.
What it has, is what we give.
Who she is, is (also) who we are.
And it is this knowing that gives birth,
To new dimensions of God

When I say, "God has no future," I mean that each one of us is a necessary component of that future. If this sounds like blasphemy to you, please know that it is not my intention to offend you or your beliefs. I simply want to be curious with you. To go on a journey of discovery in the mind of God. And why not? Is this not what we have always done? Creating more elaborate, compelling and relevant stories (boxes) to explain reality?

When people come together, for the sake of something larger than themselves without abandoning their own values and needs, what is created is something I can only describe as alchemy. This has happened thousands of times in the past. Each authentic spiritual tradition made *something from nothing* and thus expanded the mind of God.

And it is worth mentioning that holding such a perspective is significantly different than the common notion that saints and prophets received ("downloaded") a set of *divine instructions* that they merely shared with others. On the contrary, we humans and whatever you wish to call this incredible mystery that is the cosmos, go hand in hand. It has always been a reciprocal dialogue.

In my story, God does not test us.
God *needs* us.

As Jung writes, God's 'immature' behaviors originate from unconscious motives. All the evil in the world and every single act of goodness is God slowly making himself known to himself.

Think about it. Whenever you make an ethical choice, you become the teacher of God and God becomes more of itself. You are not only aligning yourself with a divine *manual for how to live a just life.* You are also becoming an active participant in the creation of a world that is more complex and nuanced.

Let this sink in for a minute: We get to create new psychological, spiritual, and cultural territories. Not discover. Create. And, with every creation, our map of reality and our stories to describe it expand. You are participating in the awakening of God. You are in a process of uncovering what is still unconscious for the sake of more God-ness.

This is what sages, leaders, scientists, thinkers, and the brave souls of the past have done. They shifted and molded consciousness, actively transforming societies. They followed the impulse. They listened to the request to dialogue with the future. They consciously or unconsciously accepted their roles as midwives for the new.

Life was created (to know itself).
God is discovering (more of) God,
which is discovering you,
Who is creating God...

This (self) discovery is as much an *ethical* process as it is a developmental one, because we are being asked to challenge our understanding of our agency in the world. Any understanding. All of our assumptions. And at the same time, include past wisdom and perspectives.

Only by having both (letting go of our understandings and holding on to past wisdom, *at once*), can greater insight and right action emerge. Our then emancipated imagination will reach the territories that rational and literal ways of knowing cannot fathom.

As cultures complexify, diversify, and individuate, so do our needs. From the one God who told us how to behave, to modern times when people carve their own truths, we are changing and maturing. This is not a *bad, better, best* process of change, but one of simple maturation.

And today many are needing socio-cultural processes that can hold the multiple perspectives they live in, *while simultaneously* focusing on the holistic aspects (in the personal domain), our global/social domains, and ecological nature of things. This sounds complicated because it is! So, no wonder that simple, populist and one-dimensional solutions, are on the rise and will continue to be until we can mature on the level of our operating system.

In order to do this, it is vital we have a better understanding of the social context of our life (which chapter five is dedicated to). But for now, let me just say that any change of perspective (or better yet, expanding perspective) should always be able to push culture to develop newer kind of *relational intelligence* — in other words, more empathy to otherness and collaboration between opposing perspectives. For our time in history, the shift that we already can see is from a binary perspective (you either agree or disagree with me) to a *yes, no, and maybe* perspective (I am right, you are right, and we both might be right or/and wrong). The shift does not require merging one perspective with the other, but of holding many perspectives simultaneously.

Among the chaos, pain, and geopolitical insanity, we are, as a species at large, at the dawn of our adulthood, being presented with a new kind of moral compass where we become responsible for ourselves, the planet, and God. Freed from the shackles of premodern religiosity, and fully aware of the limitations of the humancentric point of view and psychological traps of postmodernity, we can *create* synergies at the edge of God. This is not a top-down God where we are like children, or a bottom up God where we are the focus of our own spiritual journeys. It is a God of all directions — an orientation towards emerging worldviews, so we can co-evolve in a balance between presence, change, development, and psycho-physical health. In this way of being, we can *appropriately* respond to some of the complexities and challenges of our time.

What new myths, rituals, ceremonies, and practices would this perspective bring? What kinds of relationships would you have with others, nature, and with God when you understand your role as both the creator of the new and the creation of the past?

SOCIAL CONTEXT

Where I explain some of the reasons we are in a state of turmoil, why I believe it is the birthplace of a new kind of synergy, and what we can do about it.

5 | IN SEARCH OF A SUSTAINABLE FUTURE

Human nature is not static, nor is it finite. Human nature changes as the conditions of existence change, thus forging new systems. Yet, the earlier systems stay with us (Dr. Don Beck)

You are not as autonomous as you would like to believe. Sociologically, you are tribal. Psychologically, you are many voices in one self. You need a whole set of conditions and relationships to be a functional and well-rounded human being. Your unique self is derived from and is in relationship to the social and cultural processes that surround you. The same goes for spiritual growth—elders, mythology, initiations, wisdom teachings, contemplative practices, art, philosophy, and connections to self, others, the natural world, and a connection to spirit make it happen.

Traditionally, these conditions were offered by spiritual or religious structures as a complete package. This helped people figure out how to live in relative harmony with themselves, their communities, environment, and whatever they held to be divine or sacred. Of course, this also came with a whole bag of problems, but it did function to create a context that was bigger than the self.

This kind of cohesion is something that modern humans can only dream of, and it is almost impossible to recreate. When I teach trauma to counselling psychology students, I always remind them that our current way of living puts a lot of pressure on our biology. It is at this point in the course that I introduce the work of Bruce D. Perry, an American psychiatrist who is currently the Senior Fellow of the Child Trauma Academy in Houston. He writes:

> *For the vast majority of the last 200,000 years, humans have lived in multigenerational, multifamily hunter-gatherer bands characterized by a rich and continuous relational milieu; the concept of personal space and privacy is relatively new.... children were highly valued by the band and in these groups of 40-60 members, there were roughly four developmentally more mature potential caregivers for each child under the age of six. This enriched relational ratio helped the group protect, nurture, educate, and enrich the lives of each developing child. (p.26)*

Over the last two centuries most humans have shifted from living in small familial and clan-like groups of 40-60 members to nuclear families with three to seven members on average. More people live in big cities and small apartments than in small communities surrounded by big nature. As a result of these shifts, many have become more isolated. They have not, however, lost the need for connection and belonging.

We have substituted cohesion for choice. And we are paying a (very) high premium for that.

More than 2500 years ago, the Buddha taught that "life is suffering." Suffering may simply be a part of the human condition, yet spiritual traditions everywhere have attempted to buffer against it for millennia. However, it can't be overlooked that we are the most medicated, depressed, anxious, addicted, and suicidal generation that has ever lived on this earth.[21] Other powerful elements must be at play and they affect all of us.

Regardless of how accomplished or happy you may be, the collective pain can touch you too—your boss might be depressed, your child anxious, your neighbor addicted. Nevertheless, these concerns are still mostly dealt with on a personal level—the boss goes on medication, your child gets therapy, and your neighbor goes to a treatment center.

Our modern day existence is not completely out of synch with our biological needs. It is easy to make suffering and its treatment personal. It is easy to blame a disorder, disfunction, or disease, and to medicate, therapize, and mend the problem. But what if what we are dealing with is unsolvable on a personal level? What if our approach to ending suffering must change with our shifting times? The world is changing. Rapidly. Life has never been more dynamic, complex, and confusing. And it seems that we humans are having a somewhat difficult time adjusting. With so much social, economic, and technological change, we are not only losing biodiversity and killing the planet, but also instigating a decline in socio-cultural cohesion and resilience. Here are some alarming numbers:

- Close to 800,000 people committed suicide this year around the world.[22]
- Nearly half of all Americans report sometimes or always feeling alone (46%) or left out (47%).[23]
- Adults ages 18-22 are the loneliest generation, and claim to be in worse health than older generations.[24]
- Only about half of all Americans (53%) have meaningful in-person social interactions, such as having an extended conversation with a friend or spending quality time with family, on a daily basis.'[25]
- According to the World Health Organization, the total estimated number of people living with depression increased by 18.4% between 2005 and 2015, and the total estimated number of people living with anxiety disorders in 2015 reflects a 14.9% increase since 2005.

I think you get the idea. These numbers don't lie. There must be something else at play—something on the collective level. You might disagree with me, arguing that in general we have more freedom of choice, mental health awareness, and access to medication and therapy than ever before. This may be true, but if these measures were sufficient, why do we see more people dying from overdoses than guns and car accidents combined? Why are rates of anxiety and depression worldwide so alarmingly high?

The scope of this decline and the depth of its impact astonishes me. How detached many have become from the natural rhythms and patterns that make life manageable and meaningful. How distant some find themselves from community, nature, and spirit—and from themselves! In his brilliant article titled, "How to enslave people with addiction" Charles Eisenstein (2014) describes a setting that is eerily familiar:

> *Remove as much as possible all opportunities for meaningful self-expression and service. Instead, coerce people into dead-end labor just to pay the bills and service the debts. Seduce others into living off such labor of others... Cut people off from nature and from place. At most let nature be a spectacle or venue for recreation, but remove any real intimacy with the land. Source food and medicine from thousands of miles away... Move life — especially children's lives —indoors. Let as many sounds as possible be manufactured sounds, and as many sights be virtual sights (para 8).*

What Eisenstein is saying is that the crises of addiction, depression, and anxiety should not to be blamed *only* on people's lifestyle choices or genetic predispositions. He believes that their root cause, rather, is the profound *disconnection* people are experiencing from culture, the natural world, core needs and values, other people and community, and life essence (or call it life force, *chi*, God, spirit, higher power, Buddha-mind).

In my own personal effort to understand the causes of the suffering we see around the world today, I pursued doctoral research on addiction. I came to view addiction as a symptom of social fragmentation.[26] I proposed contemplative and ecological solutions because I saw a connection between the unmet need to belong (to self, others, nature, God) and addictive behaviors.

In my research I noticed that the more our collective anger is buried beneath the asphalt of the conscious mind (choking the earth, choking our health), the louder, larger, and more efficient our machinery of self-destruction becomes. Avoiding the real issues fuels these symptoms. This gushing force of untamed rage demands attention and it will not end until we choose to look it straight in the eyes. Unaware of the forces at play, we feed this shadow-beast with our tormented souls and earth as the offering. We become the executioner of nature, and by extension, also of ourselves.

My research led me to the ground-breaking work on dislocation of Bruce Alexander.[27] Alexander's writing helped me to develop a better understanding of the social conditions that foster disempowerment, dislocation, and alienation and the impact of rapid global change on every aspect of our lifestyle—from micro-structures like families and local institutions to macro-structures like governments and the environment.

I began to see patterns. The political, sociocultural, religious, and ecological strife we are witnessing around the world today can be viewed as the inevitable outcomes of *our psyche trying to regulate.* In other words, we seem to lack updated and relevant answers to address the relational tensions of modern life. Just look around— You can sense that when peoples' nervous systems become overwhelmed by too much change and instability, how they often collapse into conditions like depression, chronic fatigue, and general disorientation. Others shift into anxiety, panic, and/or rage. The outcomes remain the same—greater isolation, instability, and disconnection.

These symptoms not only happen on an individual level— they also effect and are affected by what can be thought of as a collective nervous system. *Society as a whole, is in the state of reactivity.* As within, so without. Robert Sardello (1982) writes:

> *The patient suffering breakdown is the world itself.... The new symptoms are fragmentation, specialization, expertise, depression, inflation, loss of energy, jargonize, and violence. Our buildings are anorexic, our businesses paranoid, our technology manic (p.75).*

Connection is so foundational to well-being that when it not met, the nervous system and emotional regulation are powerfully compromised. As a psychotherapist in private practice and the former clinical program director of an addiction treatment center, I have witnessed the pain and struggle of psychosocial dislocation up close. It is not pretty. I also witnessed what happens when people reunite with their families, heal trauma, and find spiritual connection.

Suffering adds up. In all of us — be it a trickle of discomfort or a flood of unbearable psychological pain. So many more of us are becoming isolated, and it is making us sick. In Binswanger's words, this is "the result of man's being cast out of absolute security as provided by love and loving communion into a kind of existence which is full of pain and constantly implies the danger of becoming isolated."[28] We have a choice to see this or not, but the affects, even if adjusted, will linger into the rest of the twenty first century.

THE RIGHT KIND OF PRESSURE

Just as new elements are born from the center of exploding stars, the birth of the self can be understood as the *by-product* of the *right* kind of continuous cultural pressure. What was relevant for a nomadic tribe in the Middle East in the eighth century is profoundly different from what was relevant for people who lived in medieval Paris. Each generation needs different conditions. The following questions, however, have remained relevant in every time and context:

Why am I here?

How can I be happy and avoid suffering?

What is truth?

How do I lead a moral life?

So, what happens when the cultural pressure is too weak to provide answers? Or too chaotic to offer conditions for growth? What happens when society stops offering the *right kind* of pressure?

I am going to show you what I believe can happen and how it may be affecting you both directly and indirectly. I hope that my answers will demonstrate why so many feel like misfits, why we are seeing an increase in isolation, depression, anxiety, and how this can be addressed by local, grassroots initiatives.

But first let me ask you a question: Do you feel you were provided with the right conditions to ripen and flourish as a person? To mature emotionally, intellectually and spiritually? Are you providing the right conditions for your children? When I ask around, many answer these questions with a faint "yes" or an apologetic "no."

Community is being re-birthed. In the next 10 to 20 years we will see a surge in cooperative spirituality. This pull into the *We* is slowly becoming more dominant in the public sphere—through books, podcasts, and workshops. More and more spiritual misfits will orient toward post-individualistic programs and models that offer a greater sense of belonging and fellowship. This trend is already emerging in some communities around the world (if only as a deep longing) and it will continue to build momentum and social acceptance.

However, as the pendulum swings from *I* to *We*, those who are not aware of the possibility to nurture both self (the individual) and others (belonging) may find themselves more prone to leaning into familiar collaborative formations. Ethnocentric, tribal, and authoritarian identifications will become more common. And with that, humanistic and universal values are faltering..

I worry for many — especially teenagers and young adults. There are so many offerings out there. Some are like junk food — they won't harm you, but they also won't provide spiritual nourishment. Others are more dangerous — they will suck you into an all-encompassing world that can leave you feeling hatful and resentful of others. I worry because cults, extreme political ideologies, and (fanatic) religious beliefs are on the rise. They ascend with the tides of uncertainty and instability. They gain power by feeding on people's fear and ignorance. They live in the vacuum of culture and they spread incredibly fast through social media. They can be stopped only by understanding their *social function* in an era of weak cultural pressure, great division, superficial choice, and a false sense of freedom.

We have hit a point where the speed of change (complexification and diversification) is compromising our need for stability. Our systems are shaky, which can only mean one thing — another big shift is coming.

The shift that is upon us could be good, or it could really suck. And if we don't want the latter, we first need to understand why it is so hard for us to collaborate. This is definitely not the last time that we will witness majors shifts in consciousness. It would be foolish and arrogant to think that our time is more special than any other, or that our developmental tasks are somehow more important than those of the past.

Clare Graves, a professor of psychology and the founder of a theory of adult human development called "spiral dynamics," points to the current need to change. Graves's theory was first published in an April 1974 edition of *The Futurist*, in an article titled: "Human nature prepares for a momentous leap." He color coded each stage of his spiraling developmental model to differentiate between stages and to make it easier to remember each one. It attempts to describe how and why people think about the nature of things.

Graves writes that "at each stage of human existence the adult man is off on his quest of his holy grail, the way of life he seeks by which to live." He then breaks this quest into eight levels:

§ At the first level, people are on a quest for automatic physiological satisfaction. They want to feel safe and secure [Beige]. This will usually resurface in life threatening circumstances or when one of the most basic needs are not met. The first level will always override any other level in extreme situations.

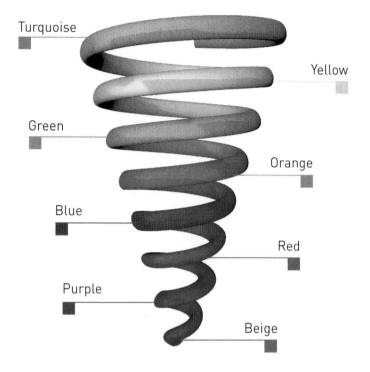

Turquoise

Yellow

Green

Orange

Blue

Red

Purple

Beige

THE SPIRAL DYNAMIC MODEL

🌢 At the second level people seek a safe mode of living [Purple]. A need to bond will emerge, together with a yearning to make sense of one's environment.

🌢 This is followed, in turn, by a heroic search for status, power and glory [Red]. Ether through taking that power for oneself or projecting that power on to a leader. Here you will see the strongest egocentric manifestations of all other levels and the rise of authoritarianism.

IN SEARCH OF A SUSTAINABLE FUTURE

§ The search for power and glory will usually be overturned by a search for ultimate peace and universal meaning [Blue]. At this stage, the well-being and success of society will override personal freedoms and choices. Loyalty, sacrifice for the greater good, and order become the highest values.

§ The tendency of blue to oppress the spirit of the individual leads into a search for material pleasure, self-governance and reason [Orange]. A more rational exploration and scientific rigor outweighs the need for ultimate peace. Society is now driven by a scientific and more humanistic worldview. Man takes the place of God.

§ The damaging aspect of Orange, such as dislocation, the deterioration of natural environments, greedy corporations, social injustice, and a general disappointment of the (grand) promise that science and democratic institutions holds the secrets to a great future, brings forth the search for affectionate relations [Green]. Here, Egalitarian values, such as diversity, self-worth, and equality, become the central force behind this worldview. Cultural hierarchies and cultural dominance are challenged, as people find solace in group identity.

§ In the next level, an integral, and emergent search for unifying principles takes central place [Yellow]. This is the first level when the individual can see all that came before. There is an eagerness to learn about self but this time with profound consideration (and care) to others. From this flexible place, the self can see how each developmental search 'for the holy grail' is important.

§ According the Graves (and since then Wilder and others have added a few more levels), the next level in the Spiral Dynamic model is the search for peace in an incomprehensible world [Turquoise]. In this level, the individual center of gravity is Cosmocentric. There is a profound acceptance of life's paradoxes and dialectics.

The spiral explains cultural conflict and geopolitical tension in a way that I have never seen before. It explains why people think about things the way they do, which can foster understanding and empathy. It gives people an opportunity to step back from their point of view to see what others see through different lenses:

Each successive state, or level of existence, is a state through which people pass on the way to other states of equilibrium. When a person is centralized in one state of existence, he has a total psychology which is particular to that state. His feelings, motivations, ethics and values, biochemistry, degree of neurological activation, learning systems, belief systems, conception of mental health, ideas as to what mental illness is and how it should be treated, preferences for and conceptions of management, education, economic and political theory and practice, etc., are all appropriate to that state. (Graves, 1974, p.2)

Take a moment to think about that. The human mind, individually and as a collective, is always evolving, becoming more adaptive and integrated. When I first read this decades ago, it blew my mind! We are not only different culturally — we are also developmentally different. This adds a new level of complexity to any attempt at collaboration because people literally do not inhabit the same psychological realities.

To put this simply, it is not that a racist or bigot does not agree with you. They experience your ideas as a threat to their world. The fundamentalist who wants to convert you (or kill you, as the case may be), perceives the world in a way that prevents him or her from understanding the concept of pluralism as a more adaptive way of being human in complex system. For progressives who cannot muster empathy for conservative points of view and who may even become enraged when somebody dares to challenge their perceptions concerning privilege, gender equality, or something else — can you see how their worldview is running *them (or you)*?

The uniqueness of Graves' model is that it does not only include personal development; it also proposes that *cultures* develop. With the emergence of each new stage of development, a new and critical aspect of consciousness is born. The older stages and representative worldviews are still around, however, and so a tension exists between the old and the new.

Until recently, we have not had the capacity to hold the perspective of a particular stage while simultaneously seeing its limitations. This is what cultural warfare was all about and why walls exist between people and nations—they express a fearful resistance to change, vulnerability, and creativity. In this era of increased psychological isolation and cultural fragmentation, many people perceive these walls of separation and the shadows they cast, but they are unsure about what to do about them.[29] This is partly because the problems we are facing are so complex and overwhelming, and partly because we face the uncharted territory of an unknown future. Cultural historian Richard Tarnas (2008) writes:

> *It is a collective dark night of the soul, a deep separation from the community of being, from the cosmos itself. We are undergoing this rite of passage with virtually no guidance from wise elders because the wise elders are themselves caught up in the same crisis (p.8).*

Our "post truth era" can be understood as (yet another) dark night of the collective soul. It can also be understood as an opportunity for growth and awakening. No one side is right, and no perspective is complete. This is both *exciting* and *terrifying* for anyone whose need for clarity, belonging, and security overrides their willingness to adapt. And there can be no clarity or security when you do not know who to trust. Because if truth depends on the developmental perspective that one inhabits, it is relative. And if truth is relative, who *can* you trust? How can you know what is right? Can you see how tempting it is to put one's trust in a charismatic, self-assured, authoritarian leader? Can you understand why people would choose loyalty to their clan over facts? Why nihilism seems like a legitimate point of view?

As life and culture become more complex, we are being asked to change. And with that push, there is an urgent need for updated structures. One way or another, adaptation (or collapse) happens—through wars, revolutions, and/or through the emergence of new ideals and fresh perspectives.

My hope is that the new cultural operating system that is emerging around the world will help us arrive at a future of our choice, not a future of our misdoings. If not, I fear, the dawn of our new day will be darkened by the storms of our worst nightmares.

BEYOND POST TRUTH

All trees grow toward the sun. If we put a barrier between the tree and the sun, the tree will continue to reach for the sun by seeking a pathway around the barrier. All humans have the same inherent impulse to grow. No matter what the obstacles are, we will move to heal, connect, develop, and find peace. When you find a barrier, you also find what needs attending to. It is always there, hiding under fear.

Bigotry, misogyny, and racism are examples of social barriers to curiosity and vulnerability. They are usually born from fear and ignorance and can change with awareness. Healthy psychological change is rarely possible or sustainable when it is forced. We know from decades of research that change is not possible when our alarm systems (like the amygdala) are activated. People do not mature when under threat or when feeling shame.

When I am confronted by "offensive" points of view or behaviors, my tactic is to become really interested in listening to what the person has to say.[30] As we have seen, when humans do not feel safe and secure, they tend to contract into more familiar and protective patterns. If a child is scared, she won't learn. When someone threatens me, I might become defensive. These reactions are not bad. They simply indicate that when we ignore developmental needs, "shadow" reactions occur.

Jung used the term "shadow" to refer to parts of ourselves that we refuse to acknowledge—repressed, avoided, disavowed thoughts, feelings, emotions, experiences, and behaviors. Our shadow is a powerful force inside our unconscious, that can spring into action when one's defenses are overwhelmed. It can be understood as anything positive, negative, or neutral that still needs to be integrated.

Shadow does not have substance.
It diminishes with awareness and clarity

As we have seen, it is impossible to destroy developmental needs. The only way forward is to meet them in the light. As culture has evolved to embrace values of diversity and pluralism, so has the counterforce, or the *shadow of inflexibility*.

Old barriers in new forms have been resurrected. Progressive ideology continues to have *in it* the counterbalanced (shadow needs) for security, clarity, and safety.

What we are witnessing is the failure of humanistic, postmodern, and pluralistic worldviews to see beyond the horizon of their own worldview.

Pluralism gave us the freedom to choose values and beliefs from different cultural, political, and spiritual sources to form our own, personalized assemblage of knowledge. This, by definition is what postmodernity is all about. The intention was to lessen cultural rigidity and reveal social blind spots. But this was not meant to be a free for all, nihilistic exploration, because in its essence pluralism seeks harmony in chaos. All of this became a problem when these philosophical positions became concrete and rigid—i.e., when a developmental stage (progressive, postmodern, pluralistic) that has its place in the spiraling context of human evolution was transformed into a value-based ideal. An unchecked truth. Wilber, in his article "Trump and a Post-Truth World," speaks to this phenomenon adeptly:

...but as the decades unfolded, [pluralism] increasingly began veering into extreme, maladroit, dysfunctional, even clearly unhealthy forms. Its broad-minded pluralism slipped into a rampant and runaway relativism (collapsing into nihilism), as the notion that all truth is contextualized (or gains meaning

from its cultural context) slid into the notion that there is no real universal truth at all, only shifting cultural interpretations (which eventually slid into a widespread narcissism) (p.4).

No matter how progressive one is, there are always hidden, unconscious aspects that need to be acknowledged and integrated. When pluralism (a system) and deconstruction (a social tool) transform into a *core value* inside a worldview — both on an individual or cultural level — extreme forms of relativism emerge and with them a post-truth attitude toward facts that can wreak havoc in society. If facts don't matter, and good is relative, then the risk of mass manipulation grows.

Deconstruction is a powerful intellectual tool. It can increase empathy for those who do not think, act, or look like us. It allowed for greater collaboration because everyone was seen to be holding a "partial but true" perspective. But there are a number of drawbacks to merging a theory (postmodern theory and deconstruction, for example) with developmental needs:

First, on a personal level, the need for individuation lacks inter-dependence, what Wilber terms "flat land." Flat in this case means that the process of maturation can become self-obsessed and self-serving because it lacks a greater context of our social destiny that includes and transcends our humanity. In a best-case scenario, one accumulates a set of principles, values, practices, and initiations that grow into an authentic lifestyle. In the worst-case scenario, the person is sucked into the vacuum of their own narcissistic projection and the echo-chamber of a compromised group identity.

Second, we flounder without a hierarchy of collective values and ideals.[31] Kellyanne Conway, an advisor to American president Donald Trump, expressed her "alternative facts" on CNN and caused an uproar because her statement was a perfect example of such a narcissistic position. The embrace of extreme relativism prevents people from connecting on the basis of ethical or moral grounds. We no longer trust a shared moral compass. As the value hierarchy has transformed into the messy truth of postmodern societies, many find themselves confused.

Third, at its very core, this worldview can become a developmental black hole. Any attempt to create a hierarchy of ideals, values, or a developmental trajectory is doomed to failure. As a result, there is no possibility (or willingness) of developing further social maps that are desperately needed. In the last twenty years or so, people who pointed this out were shamed by the dominant intellectual-ideological group. Progressive perspectives were held as dogma and those unable or unwilling to hold the same ones were seen as a threat (or as stupid). In this kind of environment, it was almost impossible for any other worldview to bring their perspective into a conversation without feeling inferior and wrong from the get-go.

Any attempt to confront this type of relativism is usually countered with agitated statements of culture, gender, or status bias. In this context, values and personal experience trump facts, for better and for worse. This means that there are fewer opportunities for collaboration beyond celebrating differences. This is specifically tragic for any effort to support genuine dialogue, especially when attempting to bring people who do not share a postmodern, relativistic worldview.

Think about it this way— The health of a rain forest is in it's diversity. Greater species diversity ensures natural sustainability for all life forms and healthy ecosystems can better withstand and recover from a variety of disasters. If you cut down most of the trees and plant only one or two types of trees, you will get a forest that is in less diverse, and therefore less immune.

So it is with our psyche. When it comes to our world, deep-diversity is a *key* factor in our collective and personal psychic strength. Without diversity— the kind that includes all of the worldviews on the spiral— consciousness is weak and more easily threatened or manipulated. Without diversity that includes hierarchy, consciousness is narrow, thus affecting our wellbeing and vitality.

Global warming, political instability, poverty, and the many other crises that we are facing on an ongoing basis will not be resolved unless we tackle the above impasse and upgrade how we think, communicate, and collaborate. It's that simple and yet tragic because this kind of *psychological leap* has very little efficacy if it stays only on the shoulders of the individual. Nor can it be supported on bigger scales (like schools or government) because our current operating system won't endorse it! What is left is the middle scale — collaborations that are not too big but not too small, at the community level, among grassroots movements.

One-dimensional solutions will not resolve the standing social issues. And to this point, the most frustrating thing is that we already have the knowledge, at least in theory, to fix most of the problems that plague us. We are blessed to have the most sophisticated theories, programs, and insights to improve wellbeing and happiness in the general population. And yet, the Western world is dealing with more depression, anxiety, loneliness, suicide and substance misuse than ever before.

A post-secular and post-individual collaborative process is so deeply needed at a time when many feel isolated, dislocated, and defended against vulnerability. The need to be able to merge worldviews with opposing ones to develop flexible minds and create new synergies is palpable. In other words, the age of fragmentation will end only when a higher order of collaborative integration emerges.

It is said that human beings long dreamed of flying, but until recently didn't have the right technology. Then in the early 1800s a community of people put their minds together to research engines and methods to control the stability of an aircraft. It took another hundred years before the Wright Brothers put all of the elements together to finally take flight. I imagine that spiritual misfits will undergo a similar journey. They are ready to take off into new frontiers of religion and culture. They know we can do better, and they are willing to experiment and make mistakes on the way.

They intuit that the new must include the past—and they will draw from the wisdom traditions of the ages and integrate science and contemporary thought easily.

No more will they separate spirit and matter, personal and collective, left and right—because they will not be as limited by the gravitational force of past worldviews and beliefs. They *will* be able to fly between them.

This, as many can sense, can be accomplished *only* through modifications in the way we *perceive and engage* reality (i.e., at the operating system level) rather than through modifications to how we *think or behave* (i.e., at the application level). So, despite the progress we have made, we currently lack the thrust we need to bring about the world we are dreaming about.

At first, you may feel overwhelmed by this vision. This is a normal reaction to any daunting task. For this reason, we must start small by undertaking localized actions, repeated again and again across many communities until they become the new normal—not a predetermined normal, but one that is born from the ground up.

As a global community, our social and personal challenges can be transformed through a deep listening to life, nature, and the divine impulse. Life calls us to re-invent ourselves as co-creators—always available for discovery, evolving, self-organizing, unifying. For we are born from and are a part of the cosmos. This means that the pulsation of a *dynamic harmony* is present in us. When we pay attention, we can see that more integration and collaboration are critical to the future of culture. Although none of us knows what constitutes truth or right action, we can at least inquire into the needs, beliefs, motivations, goals, and values of people and community—one community at a time.

There will be a need for updated structures that can hold our level of complexity, structures that will be able to mold diversity into a new type of integrative, relational experience. These socio-cultural structures will hold multiple perspectives while simultaneously focusing on the developmental arch of life. Our collective achievements will be used as building blocks where dialectics, not opposition, are the guideposts. The combination of multiple perspectives arising *at once* will create rich, local tapestries from which new insights and hopefully, solutions, will emerge.

In these new formations, great attention will be paid to personal, spiritual, and cultural orientations and psychological development in the interest of fostering collaborative, synergistic dialogues. Gone are the days when we only focus on spiritual growth or psychological health. The new dialectic of the divine will allow the trappings of each point of view to be seen, appreciated, and transcended.

The impulse that moves through us as the whole spiral of consciousness will be collective because there is too much for any individual to integrate on their own. These new formations will not dismiss or diminish individual needs or group identity, but they also will not get stuck only on personal experience and cultural perspectives.

A new relational balance will breed a way of being together that can integrate the divine and the human, the one and the many. This collective impulse will create a new consciousness—one that is still mostly unknown. For me, this is not wishful thinking or a utopian dream. We are ready for this.

PART
TWO

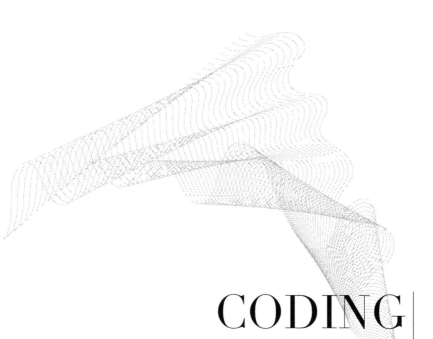

CODING

*Where I explain the mechanisms of the
CODE, and how you can use it in
your community.*

—

At the event horizon of God's evolution,
what will I see?
I don't know!
Who I am now,
will not exist then.

But I do know that
the fabric of spacetime will twist
and things
will get crazy.

My light is drawn
By the force of his gravity,
To serve.

6 | A COMPREHENSIVE ORIENTATION

I t was Friday morning. I was sitting on my favorite couch in my favorite café, drinking my favorite drink (a latte, if you want to know). Just as I did on any other Friday, I was writing in my journal, trying to bring all of the fragmented pieces I had been working on for almost two years together. The idea that it might actually click into a model hadn't even occurred to me, but something surprising happened that morning. Everything made sense. I discovered a model. It was practical and, more importantly, simple.

After many modifications, conversations, and community dialogues, I stumbled upon a "good enough" draft model that I was proud to share with others—something that could bridge spiritual wisdom and contemporary scientific understanding with psychological insight, creating a flexible and coherent model. It presents a way of *being* as opposed to a construct. It serves as an information-processing system or set of psycho-spiritual algorithms that can decrypt cultural data. And it tries to capture the spiral, cyclical, multi-directional dance of humans, nature, and God.

DEVELOPMENTAL TASKS	SPIRITUAL ELEMENTS	ORGANIZING PRINCIPLES
Orient: Engage from safety. **Play:** Orient from pleasure. Lean into safety. **Actualize:** Play with agency. Lean into pleasure **Connect:** Actualize love. Lean into agency **Communicate:** Connect to Communicate. Lean into love. **Plan:** Communicate your common vision. Lean into communication. **Execute:** Plan your action. Lean into vision.	**Practices (and rituals)** **Questions** **Ceremonies** **Initiations (and rights of passage)** **Stories and mythologies**	**Holism:** The great way (Antidote to isolation) **Rhythm:** The pulse of life (Antidote to dysregulation) **Creativity:** When everything goes (Antidote for fear) **Presence:** Tapping into what is already perfect (Antidote to suffering) **Balance:** 'Yes, no and maybe…?' (Antidote to rigidity)

The Comprehensive Orientation for Developmental Emergence (CODE) presents the possibility of seeing beyond our current horizons. Only structures that are capable of naturally flowing between static answers, a developmental worldview, and collaborative wisdom will be embraced by the misfits who are seeking God but are unwilling to engage in hierarchical dogma.

The CODE can support any kind of community you are part of or want to build. It is modular and adaptive so that it can be used in already established religious contexts (e.g., churches, synagogues, mosques, or temples) and by more eclectic, pluralistic entities. Whether your group deems itself religious, spiritual, agnostic, atheistic, or all of the above, the model will enable you to visualize and then engage with the basic source code of the model. It provides clarity and guidelines with as little agenda as possible. You can choose to integrate the whole model or only parts of it (Or just be inspired by it and create your own variation).

No two versions of the CODE will look the same. Each community will choose its own practices, initiations, ceremonies, and interventions based on the specific lineages and cultural backgrounds present. It is up to the group to find the right balance between (1) maintaining a collaborative process, while (2) addressing the individual needs of members, and (3) orienting toward emerging divinity.

The main purpose of the CODE is to create the conditions for collaboration. Conditions. Not answers, or even a direction. These conditions will help you and your community create *your own version* or story of the future of God (if in your version God even has a future, or even an existence). My greatest hope is that its implementation will happen as organically as possible.

Below I share the architecture of the CODE. Even if you don't grasp it after your first reading, it will come alive through practice. As you go through the CODE's process, you may believe you are missing something. You are not. I purposefully didn't give too much direction or tools. I wanted it to be yours—because you know this innately. You are the CODE in your own way—you are a whole and a part, you have inherent rhythms and balance. You are profoundly creative and your nature is already in utter, peaceful presence at all times.

And besides, you are not doing this alone. What you need to know will be found in the diverse wisdom and resources of your community. Just give it time *and* follow the basic ground rules I propose.

This is a process of co-creation. Trust that a unique set of insights will arise from the creative tension in your group. It will surprise you, just as it did me that Friday morning while I drank my latte.

THE (DEVELOPMENTAL) PROCESS OF THE CODE

How do you start?
What should be your first step?
What should you be aware of?

The first answer is that there really are no strategies available, because what you are about to do has never been done before. Oh, how my editors hated that I expressed this reality. But it's true. No one has done this because your unique community—what it will unveil and how it will collaborate—is original. At no time in human history have we had the opportunity to be so radically free to think and be who we are, and also have the critical insight to grasp the limitations of our freedom.

You are about to take a leap into the event horizon of God. Don't let it go to your head, but also acknowledge that even your willingness to take this leap is a big deal. We desperately need new insights to get us out of the mess we're in, and I can't think of a safer, more respectful or playful way to achieve them.

This process will unfold, grow, evolve. There is no end that you are trying to arrive at. Rather, you are entering into a living relationship that will have ups and downs. So, I ask you to please keep in mind that enlightenment is not your destination. Healing is not about fixing yourself. Personal growth is not about perfecting your life. If anyone in your community is selling these ends, walk away. The last thing you need is (another) homogenous spiritual community living according to pregiven dogma and believing themselves to be cutting edge. Besides, the CODE is not about doing something new just for the sake of being new. This tendency is another trap that needs to be noticed and avoided.

I once met a person who wanted to leave her community. She was summoned into a room with more advanced students. She was told that her ego was standing in the way of her spiritual growth. She almost second-guessed her impulse to leave, but in the end decided to go. A week later, the community collapsed, and many members were hurt emotionally. This kind of emotional manipulation is something that can happen, so I dedicated a chapter in the end of Part two to the dangers of spiritual communities. We do not need another friendly cult. Your community may be a cool, funky, and a super progressive cult. But it is still a cult.

If you suddenly suspect that your tribe is turning cultish, raise a red flag. Speak up. Explore your concerns with other members. Question the collective leadership. Debate power and own your own shadows. The fantasy of a spiritual destination, of a perfect community, of fixing yourself—it's all a dangerous delusion. It can lead people on a perverted spiritual expedition that ultimately only produces more self-doubt, resentment, and confusion. Instead, see these aspirations as a manifestation of an unmet developmental need that is seeking completion through the wrong means.

From years of research on this subject and from my personal experience, I can testify that we usually need much more practice (and thus time) than we think we do to integrate a new skill or task. Building healthy, long-lasting, and sustainable relationships takes time. There have been too many attempts to jump straight into vision or action when the psychological foundations of the community are still too shaky. Most communities that start this way do not last. Collaborative work is too risky and complex to justify taking shortcuts. I am emphasizing this because there is no point in striving to align yourself with a collaborative vision if there is risk that you and/or the people around you may be traumatized or hurt due to ignorance and impatience.

This is the heart of the model!
Go back to move ahead,
Slow down to build speed.

You should never feel that you are only here to achieve some abstract, bigger and better future. If you do, sound the alarm! There are so many examples of well-intentioned groups that ended in tragedy, of communities whose charismatic leaders or rigid ideology stripped its members of their individuality.

Followers who do cut off contact with friends or family are risking their mental, emotional, (and sometimes) physical health for the group.

So, if the experience feels familiar, it's not new, and co-creation has stopped.

Therefore, I have developed a process that maps the developmental trajectory of individuals and collectives. To put this differently, you and your group are *developmental entities*. The group is not only the container for personal work. It is also a *reason* for collaboration — for consciousness (or God) to know itself as more than the individual.

The CODE will support the development of a group of individuals who are willing to hold both their unique viewpoints *and* a collective perspective without collapsing into a group mentality. So, what you will experience is a double helix of growth:

Personal growth *and* a collective journey.
The individual woven into an evolving group, at once.

You are about to spiral into a higher tier capacity while actually turning back into the beginning of our journey as humans. The same journey our ancestors took more than 50,000 years ago is now being asked of you to be walked again, but this time with an awareness of all that has come before you.

When the developmental process is slow and steady, something fresh, and still unknown, emerges. The insights and integration in your community are going to be distinct from any other group or institution that is using the CODE.

One community might be mostly Christian with some members being atheist or non-religious, while another community might be mostly Buddhist with a few non-sectarian Jewish and Muslim members. Some communities will have no affiliation with any religion or even a clear spiritual path. Others will want to use the CODE as a way to build a secular, contemplative community.

Because the CODE is an open-source model, I encourage you and the leadership team to do your own research. Develop an adaptation of the CODE that works for your community. There are other developmental models that take our ecological, spiritual, and psychological needs into consideration, while remaining cognizant of our biases. Some have created unique symbioses of East-West philosophy, while others are oriented toward soul-work, indigenous perspectives, or an ecological point of view.

By the time you finish this process, you and your community will have the tools and skills to answer some of the most pressing questions of our time:

1. How can we increase our sense of safety and belonging in the midst of polarized, dislocated cultural contexts?
2. How do we give ourselves permission to explore all of our ideas, needs, values, and perceptions without being

shamed, marginalized, or becoming overwhelmed?

3. How do we actualize power and share it with others? Is power a limited resource?

4. How do we embody more love in our lives and in our relationships with others—human and non-human? What can we do to feel more connected to ourselves, others, nature, and God?

5. How can we communicate our ideas, worldviews, and needs in genuine, respectful, and compassionate ways?

6. How can we develop and share a common vision, where no one needs to compromise and where everyone can bring their full emerging selves as active participants?

7. How does it feel to bring all that we learn into our family life, work environment, education, governance, art, and play?

THE SEVEN YEAR CYCLE
OF THE CODE

In the Hasidic movement, there is a great saying: *The fast path is slow and the slow path is fast.* This easily remembered proverb points to a very important truth:

There is no shortcut for doing things well.
Growth takes time.

There are no weekend workshops, programs, or retreats that will give you the same satisfaction as a long, progressive, developmental process that involves building community.

This is why the CODE is a *seven-year* process...
It is a really, really, slow pursuit, with an *end*.
Because all that is alive, must die.

When was the last time you heard of a spiritual community that has an expiry date? This is one of the elements that makes the CODE unique. It honors the spiritual process, but also sees stagnation as a danger. It finds a balance between holding the great traditions in check by composting the container of spiritual work every seven years. When spiritual communities hold on to their ideals, leadership, and spiritual path for too long, foundational beliefs become distorted. I will say more about this danger in Chapter ten.

A seven-year commitment seems impossible in our fast-paced era, where instant gratification is expected. People find it hard to commit to a *weekend* training or retreat, let alone a seven-year process. Now, it doesn't *have* to be seven years, but this would be my recommendation. The timeline will be different for everyone and depends largely on your goals. You can go through the tasks in one year or even in a few weeks. All I am saying is that you get the best chance for success if you allow each task to mature over time. The bigger the structure, and the more moving pieces involved, the slower you want to take it. If you are using the CODE just for your family, you can probably circle around the tasks every few months; but if you are using it for a larger group (let's say more than 20 people), then I urge you to take a whole year for each task.

Without dedicated practice, repetition, and peer support, it is unlikely that any behavior will become a habit, let alone a core aspect of your evolving personality. Because of the nature of the human mind, its tendencies and shadows, and our current cultural conditioning, there is need for a collaborative process that guides us as we transition from a more singular worldview to a synergistic worldview. This will take a long time. The new structures that emerge will be wholly new and localized, and therefore will bring a fresh understanding of right-action, values, and cooperation. This is not something that anybody can teach you, because it has never been done before. The process and outcome will be uniquely your own.

The CODE is radical because it is so slow. It will be difficult to implement, and this might turn you off. But anything less will not give the community the kind of process that allows all of its members to mature organically.

Let me explain, Lacking mature, emotionally and mentally healthy members, the group will not readily create its own vision and then act upon that vision sustainably. This is why it's best to take a substantial amount of time (almost three years) to ensure that all members have established adequate psychological flexibility.[32] This groundwork will support the paradigm shift you are after.

This is why the first three tasks/years in the process focus on psychospiritual development as groundwork (orienting toward self); the next two tasks/years focus on building relationships (orienting toward the each other); and the last two tasks/years focus on supporting that vision to take off (orienting toward change). Each year leans on the developmental task of the passing year and uses the five principals as a guideline. It flows like this:

GROUNDWORK (year one to three)

Year 1 (Orient): Engage from safety. Dedicated to establishing a sense of grounding and relational safety for all its members.

Year 2 (Play): Engage from pleasure. Lean into safety. Focused on self-exploration, and re-orientation to pleasure.

Year 3 (Actualize): Engage from agency. Lean into pleasure. The discovery of self-agency and choice.

PREPARATION (year four and five)

Year 4 (Connect): Engage from love. Lean into Groundwork. Explore deeper love and attachment styles.

Year 5 (Communicate): Engage from communication. Lean into love. Embody nonviolent communication among members.

TAKEOFF (year six and seven)

Year 6 (Plan): Engage from vision. Lean into Preparation. Reflect on the uniqueness of the community and develop its vision.

Year 7 (Execute): Engage from action. Lean into vision. Put into place new insights. Take action in the world.

Then, circle back.

You can see how the tasks appear and re-appear in each year. Naturally, they do not stand alone! But the heightened awareness of dedicating a year for each task allows these developmental needs to find deep roots in each person.

The CODE starts with the most basic human need— for emotional and physical safety. It then moves from one developmental need to the next, always building on the focus of the previous element before proceeding. So, if things get too stirred up, you can find comfort in what you are already familiar with. All members and the group as a whole move through the developmental journey *together*.

If you wish to build healthy communities and truly come together, you need to start by establishing grounding, presence, and safety (Orientation). Thereafter, you can enter securely into your inner world (Play), which will allow you to get to know your unique self and its one-of-a-kind perspective on reality (Direct). Through knowing yourself, you can truly meet and come to love others

(Connect). And when human beings come together with this capacity, they can communicate with love and express their common ground, values, and uniqueness in community (Communicate). Only then — and this is where communities lapse into discord or even collapse — will you hold a vision large enough (Plan) for fruition to emerge (Execute).

And this is what it means to fly into the inner space of relationships — to build a new kind of us that truly honors the personal and the collective.

Spending a full seven years to complete one developmental cycle of the CODE engages the virtue of perseverance and the patience of God. Time should be viewed as a key. By slow-cooking the process, there is ample opportunity for members and for the group as a whole to address unmet developmental needs.

As society today speeds up, people's lives are spiritually, emotionally, and even physically undernourished. Spending a full year on each developmental step of the CODE will allow you to align the rhythms of your *animal body,* the part of you that is in actual participation with the world, with the speed of today's *digital world.*

The pulse of time reminds you to pay attention to the weeks, months, and years that always spiral back to beginnings, dancing with nature, moving forward and coming back to an old-new starting point. Communities can lean into what is always available in nature. When you give yourself time each day throughout the year to know yourself and others, you can move from an intellectual to an embodied understanding.

This is where you can be alone and miss nothing,
where the silence of nature enlivens you,
where you are present.

Our ancestors knew:
only through the passing of the seasons,
can you feel timeless.[33]

INTEGRATING SPIRITUAL ELEMENTS WITH CODE

Before we jump into the manual of working with the CODE, I would like to take a minute to speak about integrating spiritual elements in your community. It's a touchy subject and in the end, it will be up to your community to decide on the right balance.

All authentic spiritual traditions have developed a set of tools for personal salvation, healing, awakening, and answering our greatest questions. They have helped humanity for millennia to undertake the humble work of prayer and play as presented by each premodern religion.

For the sake of simplicity, I have identified five core "spiritual elements," including practices, indestructible questions, ceremonies, initiations, and stories. I left the elements content-free because it is not up to me to know what works for you and your community. The content of the elements does not really matter, as long as they support the principles and follow a developmental process in alignment with the law of your country. At some point, your community will develop its own traditions and ceremonies.

Lastly, you must be wary of any element that has a cohesive quality. It is easy to manipulate ourselves (and others) to act in ways that do not feel right. I ask you to take responsibility for your spiritual process and to pay close attention to power differentiation. In addition, notice when an element is being used just because it's part of a lineage but holds no value to you. Please keep the tension between the dogma of your lineage and the freedom to choose—debate with others and decide for yourself what's right for you. As a general rule, it is always good to start with elements that provide safety and healthy boundaries and move from there to more risky ones.

Practices: Any activity or strategy that is intended to increase a person's and/or a community's well-being through establishing new healthy habits. They can be as simple as a gratitude list or as complex as elaborate visualizations. Spiritual and psychological practices can establish a healthier relationship with both self and others (the *other* here includes the natural world), and a (re)integration with what remains unexpressed and yet painfully disturbing to the self—i.e., the shadow of the personal and collective unconscious mind.

Indestructible Questions: What is love? Why are we here? What is the meaning of my life? What is the right thing to do? These questions demand your full attention when you engage them because the answers they produce are alive. They should be embodied through your life and actions. The answers you find are never complete, because the questions are relational—they happen in the now, alongside others.

Ceremonies: A repeated, formal, and seasonal spiritual event, usually with art-based elements. Ceremonies can be understood to be connecting activities that bring people together. Ceremonies frame life, and thus create a spiral continuity through the seasons and years to help you connect with others through agreed, culturally approved, meaning-making exchanges.

Initiations: Initiations are unique and personal rituals that access your vast inner life or connect with the more-than-human world—with the soul or the divine. These can be understood as transformational thresholds which pivot people into a new emerging level of development. Initiations are based on a process that facilitate alignment to what is already available for you at any given moment: a basic intelligence that is at the core of life and who you are.

Initiations are used as gateways to heightened states of consciousness, as a means to examine future stages of development or to explore primordial fears and terror.

Stories: Stories and mythologies are founded on core archetypes that reside in the unconscious of humankind, influencing feelings, experiences and behavior on all levels of culture. Stories and mythologies define, create, and even destroy societies. They are linked to the symbolic dimension of our psyche, helping us to explore elements of human existence. These stories include core aspects of our humanity, of cultural and divine existence.

FINDING YOUR TRIBE
WITH THE CODE

We are all looking for our tribe[34]—a place to belong on the most primal, biological level. We seek a place where our whole self is welcomed. But I don't believe we are able to recreate a structure—the tribe, the clan—that is long gone. Torn by the afflictions of civilization, we are left mostly alone in the world, thrown into a terrifying existence that offers us far reaching freedom *and* fewer deep, nourishing connections. *But*—and this is a huge but—our biology doesn't know this. We are born tribal and we will continue to seek the tribe until we die.

So, *synthetic* tribal living is all we have
and it is something you can create with others.

For spiritual misfits, this means *re-integrating* the fabric of
your lives into a social structure that can hold your complex
stories. You can embrace a sense of belonging in a diverse
environment without losing any part of yourself in the group.
The CODE is a group process that ideally should include
between 15 to 250 members. This is "Dunbar's range",
which suggests that there is a cognitive limit to the number
of people with whom you can be in relationship, without
losing social stability.

One error to which nascent spiritual organizations are
prone is attempting to broaden their vision to reach ever-
greater numbers of adherents. While aiming to make a big
impact is honorable, I maintain that a small-scale focus is best
for collaborative spirituality. While it may indeed be *possible*
to envision and execute a much larger scale, like a national
or global organization, at this point in time, any spiritual
structure that is larger than a tribe will not be long-term
sustainable and eventually will fracture into smaller groups,
ultimately weakening the capacity of the group to embody
the original impulse.[35]

For what is needed *today*, the CODE's bottom-up approach
proposes that communities focus on the maturation of group
members and on building a cooperative vision that harnesses
the unique synergies of each and every community. Each
micro-community will orient toward itself, circling in, from

year to year—not to isolate but to build capacity on a small scale in order to handle incredible amounts of diversity and complexity in a *stable* and *ongoing* manner. That by itself is already a highly complex social leap that rarely happens.

Although the local, adaptive, and developmental microstructures of the CODE can embrace ideas from all disciplines and worldviews, the process and outcomes should be distinct from tribe to tribe—no grand solutions or meta-theories, but instead a unique synergistic flow between universal, humanistic, cultural, individual, and tribal values. This means that each tribe should maintain a clear holarchy of their own ideas, needs, and values as members discover the delicate balance between the personal and the collective, groups and tribe, and distinctive lineages.

Each tribe will focus on different aspects of spiritual and religious life, as it manifests through them, while they simultaneously (1) support each member of the tribe with their individuation process; (2) engage in dialogue among the diverse lineages in the tribe; and (3) take part in intra-tribal dialogue.

I trust that with enough integrity, a diverse leadership structure and a strong lineage base, combined with the principles, elements, and developmental process, each tribe will be able to celebrate one or more micro-variation on the endless theme that is the learning and growing God.

A WORKING MANUAL FOR A CO-CREATIVE DANCE WITH GOD

This is where you begin to actually explore using CODE. While the structure may seem linear, you will find it to be messy and organic in practice. To make it easier to work with the manual, I have divided the seven tasks into three clusters which are explored consecutively in the following three chapters:

Years 1-3 (Groundwork), which I title The I Project.
Years 4-5 (Preparation), which I title From Me to We.
Years 6-7 (Takeoff), which I title Insights and Fruition.

Enjoy the ride...

7 | GROUNDWORK: THE 'I' PROJECT (YEAR ONE TO YEAR THREE)

The first three tasks of the CODE invite you to become intimate with how you feel, think, act; how you play, find safety, and connect to your power. This, on its own, is not new. Personal work, be it spiritual or psychological, has been part of the human story for millennia. However, the context is unique. You are establishing the groundwork for collaborative spirituality, for the integration of your personal growth with a significant developmental leap on a collective level.

Dedicate *year one* to contemplation and grounding practices and, through the five spiritual elements, discover new resources that can strengthen existing ones. Do it within your lineage or through the bigger gatherings of your tribe. Take your time and notice if you or others are moving too fast. The first year is also for the tribe to slowly gather and orient to one another. With enough groundwork, *year two* will bring healthier risks and playfulness. Using art-based inquiry and initiations can amplify the process throughout the first three years.

Year one is intended to establish ground and safety, and year two is about play and the pleasure of exploration; *year three* will be the culmination of *grounded pleasure* and *safe play* for each member. Two years of exploration will bear the fruit of self-discovery. You and others will loosen unexamined cultural conditioning in year two and open yourself to self-love and acceptance, so that healthy discrimination and actualization flourish.

The first three years should embrace a slow and *organic* process. Please do not rush. The slower the process, the more you will see into the fabric of your reality. I encourage you to take as much time as you need to explore the topics of safety, resources, permission, and power with ease, curiosity, and a lot of patience. Insights, even profound ones, need time to establish roots, and this is especially true with collaborative work. Spending this time will be rewarding. Safety and vulnerability will grow. Curiosity will flourish. Transformation will emerge.

In the process of knowing yourself, you will listen to your inner multiplicity and re-connect to who you are. And if we are working with the nonlinear, unpredictable aspect of our consciousness, is it not appropriate to speak its mythological and imaginative language? Is it not our ethical responsibility to *speak in tongues* to our multifaceted psychic life? So *listen* as leaves listen and *be* as rocks are.

Year one to three embodies the activity of disruption; we disturb the status quo of our lives, masks that we wear, and social conditions that we do not question. Only then can we begin to dive into the deep waters of our soul.

Imagine going diving in a location that has never been explored. You are going to need the right equipment and the proper training. This is what the first three years of the CODE provide. If the transpersonal is the unfolding mystery of the impulse, then consider knowledge of self and your communication skills to be that equipment.

It is easy for communities, especially spiritual ones, to focus on ascending into higher realms and transpersonal states. It is tempting to ignore or leave behind necessary though uncomfortable and painful psychological work and to bask instead in the sun of the divine.

I have been part of so many groups that believed that their intellectual understanding would fare them well in the stormy waters of the collective mind. But that was never the case. No one can avoid the messy, vulnerable, painful, and confusing parts that long-term group work inevitably stirs up. People will trigger each other. Words, unintentionally, will hurt. Some will collapse into shame while others will retaliate—if not openly, then through vindictive, judgmental, and cruel thoughts that can be felt if not heard. This is part of our conditioning and no amount of goodwill or spiritual ideals can overcome this.

So please…

No big visions. Avoid talking about anything people might consider to be ideological in the tribe. Keep this to your own group or lineage. Your main job in the first three years, as a group, is to support each other to do deep *personal* work. And no one can (really) tell you how to do *you*. No one. At the same time, keep in mind the trajectory of the tribe as a whole — moving slowly into collaboration and embracing ambiguity while maintaining a search for unity. In the end, I wish for you to enjoy both worlds — where you fall in love with yourself *and* see your place in the evolution of your community.

HOW TO START A COMMUNITY USING THE CODE

I am going to assume that the call to action is burning inside you. I'm also going to guess that you have already had some conversations about this topic. This book is an invitation for you to get together with friends and family and undertake more of these conversations.

To begin, maybe invite people who you know might care about this subject and start a conversation online or, better, in person. You could begin with a book club and use this book. The process should work for you, so as long as you follow the general parameters of the CODE or some parts of it, it's all good!

Try to introduce the CODE early in year one, but don't get too heady. Your main goal in the first few months is to establish a respectful and safe space. The developmental process, contemplative elements, and principles of the CODE will be your guide. However, the journey is yours to walk. Eventually, a website with resources and forums will be established to share insights and ideas, and to support you with troubleshooting. Being an open-source model, collaborative initiatives will emerge spontaneously.

Early stage leadership: In the beginning, the leadership team should include people who are trained in group facilitation and conflict resolution. This will minimize normal but unnecessary tensions in the early stages of group formation.[36] Be wary of anyone who is too eager to implement their version of the vision, or of anybody who is pushing to take charge. They are going to be either a powerful force for good or a liability, depending on whether the community keeps them accountable and in check.

Make sure that there is a gender balance in the leadership team and, as much as possible, avoid having power couples and charismatic personalities take charge, especially if they declare some sort of special or spiritual status. Until conversations about how to choose the leadership have occurred, the lineage holders can take their place as the temporary leadership team. The leadership should be firmly established by the end of year two.

Gatherings: The tribe meets as many times as the community wants. A weekly gathering would be a good start. Other dedicated gatherings for each lineage and distinctive groups should be formed — e.g., inner work groups, women or men's groups, therapeutic groups, mindfulness training, parents and couple support groups, and so on. The gatherings should feel pleasurable, playful, and creative!

Lineage integration: As more people gather in the first several months, the major lineages and groups of the tribe will form. These can be composed of anything from three to the maximum participants per tribe (which I recommend should not surpass 250 people).

Feedback and honesty: Giving feedback is common in spiritual circles, but please encourage people to *check before they wreck* the blooming of new relationships. Many early-stage communities overwhelm members; those who can't handle too much feedback, or who need a gentler approach, will probably leave the group if this practice is unchecked. Eventually, the group will become homogenous. For those in the tribe who long for more intense feedback (or radical honesty), I recommend a separate process group where radical honesty can be practiced. No one needs to give up what they want; nothing has to be compromised. For feedback to be productive, there's a need for rapport, love, and skillful non-violent communication — all conditions that take time to cultivate. I recommend that no unsolicited feedback be given in the first two or even three years. This includes intense opinions, strong feelings about each other, or unchecked gossip.

Not sharing feedback is a skill unto itself, because it will force you to get to know your inner dialogues and automated reactions when your emotional triggers are pushed. Developing the skill to orient back to the self by taking responsibility is exactly what the first years are about. With enough open curiosity, support, and awareness, you will learn to comprehend your needs and communicate those needs with clarity and compassion.[37] This, of course, does not mean that you should not ask for what you need, have clear boundaries, or keep others accountable. What you are after is a balance between honesty and empathy. Too much honesty leads to cruelty. Too much empathy stunts change and growth.

Non-centralized process: The CODE is not a centralized process. Each tribe, every lineage and group, and every member has complete autonomy with regard to how to engage the process. There is no right way of working with the CODE. Each community can be unique in their explorations, practices, initiations, and ceremonies. This allows for a *responsibility tier* that starts with the individual, then the group, next lineage, and eventually the whole tribe. Each tier of responsibility carries power differently and therefore becomes a point of reference in the balancing act of the non-centralized process.

Imagine a tribe that includes a Catholic lineage, an atheist group, and a small Buddhist *sangha*. They come together to celebrate diversity and accept differences, and they work toward a new localized collaborative spirituality that produces unique insights after they have spent a significant amount of time together. If done well, there would be mutual respect, friendship, and understanding, and a way of being and doing that can be shared with others. The developmental process can protect the independence of each and every member, the established rules, values and ideals of the lineages, and the self-government of each tribe.

This process can be demanding and complex. The added layers of complexity can be overwhelming. This is why each tribe is asked to adjust the developmental process to fit their own members. They also always start with the most basic of tasks—ensuring that all members feel safe, grounded, and connected.

The CODE allows members to understand that no matter how progressive, inclusive, truthful or advanced the perspectives being held may be, they are still never complete. Every perspective can be integrated and challenged. All of the perspectives in the tribe have limited power, and there will be no felt need for one worldview to attack or deconstruct others. For example, diversity in this model can be understood as a value of a specific developmental worldview and not a universally held goal that needs to be achieved by the whole community, so members can reject this notion within their lineage and embrace it in their tribe.

This means that each tribe must hold a dialectical tension between the heterogeneous nature of the tribe and the homogenous qualities inside each lineage and developmental worldview. This allows for any perspective to be appreciated and integrated, even if it means that only one person or a specific lineage in the tribe holds that perspective. Minority perspectives are then heard and respected as a position without the tyranny of the circle, where one does not feel that they are allowed to speak their truth if it goes against the group.

It will hopefully allow members to see how each and every point of view has value, if only to point back to the essence of the holonic and evolving nature of all perspectives. In this scenario, each and every perspective becomes the center from which the world can be understood, and at the same time there is freedom to shift, play, and even reject perspectives. This is the win-win nature of the CODE.

Non-centralized leadership: Have you ever fallen in love with somebody's writing, vision, or energy so much that you decided to change your life? So much that you had to re-think who you are? Did you ever join a group or community because of that person?

These are experiences that I am familiar with, and I'm lucky that they had a positive impact on my life. But I also saw the danger of giving my power to ideas and people. I witnessed how many of my friends had unrealistic expectations of their leaders.

If you look closely, even spiritual organizations that have a board of directors or a group of influential members hold an orientation toward a singular leadership position— be it a person, a notion of God, a vision, an ideology, or a worldview. Even pluralistic and multicultural spiritual groups operate according to a specific worldview that has relativism as its core.

It is so tempting to buy in to other people's ideas, some of which may be fantastic! There are those among us— trailblazers, innovators, spiritually mature beings—who hold a unique understanding that needs to be shared with the world. How can you welcome their leadership in your life without allowing them to become an idealized authority in your mind? The CODE invites people to imagine spiritual communities where the leadership is not bound by one ideology, tradition, or a powerful leader.

The CODE offers a different leadership model, wherein communities embrace premodern, modern and postmodern models of leadership all at once! Together with the growing fields of psychology, art, science, and systems theory, the CODE challenges any notion of what leadership is and invites you to rethink notions of power. Conversations about power and leadership need to move from predictable and known answers into a holonic, dialectic, and developmental dialogue.

This is not an approach most of us are familiar with. By using the principles, elements, and processes, it will become relevant for each and every lineage within your tribe and for the tribe at large to know what your leadership will look like. I ask you to take into consideration some of the main attributes that will guide you in your own leadership process. For now, I would like to offer a multilayered type of leadership as a guideline. This leadership is thus an amalgamation of:

Personal leadership: Leadership is understood as ownership over one's life. You are encouraged to take responsibility not only for your power, identity, needs, and values, but also for your natural capacity to lead by example—to identify wrongdoing on one hand and to let go of rigidity on the other. Through the journey of self-development, you learn to actualize your core positions in the context of your evolving community.

Group as leadership: This is a shift from one active group leader into a view of leadership as a dynamic, alive *presence* that all members are part of. When guided by this kind of leadership, the group listens to what can be described as a leadership impulse that may arise in different members, at different times. Wisdom, as it manifests through the members, is understood as a non-personal, rotating, hierarchical force that anyone can access at any moment.

Lineage holders: Those who have developed mastery and wisdom can be called lineage holders. These elders provide connection to the depths of their tradition/s.

The lineage holders add the specific point of view of each tradition by providing stories, anecdotes, moral guidelines, and rules. This type of leadership may vary significantly between each tribe in relationship to the different worldviews each tribe may hold.

A leadership team: The tribe will have a leadership team that includes representatives from each lineage and group. A *minimum* of four individuals would be my recommendation, and ideally there would be a balance of genders (two or more women and two or more men).

It is the mutual responsibility of all four types of leadership and the community at large to notice, name, and work with power, choice, and projections. Corruption, unhealthy sexual dynamics, financial scandals, and the blurring of boundaries can erupt at any time. This natural phenomenon can be minimized if people speak about power as it resides in themselves, their group, and in the tribe. And please remember that even these conversations can be manipulated to control members, so be aware.

Lastly, let's talk about money and community; The financial structure of each community is its own business. However, if the community can afford a salary for its leadership team, then try to cap the annual income at a reasonable level. This will reduce the risk of financial corruption and increase trust.

Many outstanding communities (and friendships) have fallen apart due to complicated and unethical relationships with money. Whatever model you choose, the conversation about how the community uses its resources should be ongoing.

YEAR ONE: Orientation | Safety
Resourcing, and grounding

- Orient to what makes you feel safe
- **Measure of success:** Does everyone feel safe?
- **Questions for group members to explore:** Are the meetings light and inviting? Are you safe in your body? How do you know? Are you okay with other people in the group?
- **You are ready for the next year when...** People know how to find their ground as a felt sense (Gendlin, 1982); they have resources and practical tools; they can communicate to others if they cross the threshold of their emotional ability. In other words, they know and can tell people around them that they are not feeling safe.
- **Trouble spots:** The process becomes lifeless or too slow; safe spaces are used to avoid tough conversations and people; safety as control; safety becomes an intellectual concept.

No ground, no stability.
This is your mantra for year one.

◇◇◇◇◇◇◇◇◇◇◇◇

Safety is the ground upon which life blossoms and thrives. Long-term sustainable growth is not possible without equilibrium, and equilibrium is only established when our (animal) body feels safe. It is not enough to know you are safe with others. Of course, you (mostly) are! But it is another matter to know it from your body. Our bodies carry trauma, bad memories, slights, and rejections. They live in the now but constantly refer to their past experiences. Teaching the body to feel safe enough with others takes time.

Safety is an act of mutual responsibility, and a nuanced balance between too little and too much emotional change. It requires a willingness to attend to the moment to moment needs of each person, along with an acceptance of continuous shifting. There will be times of openness and times when people will shut down.

Without the foundation of safety, it is extremely difficult to become intimate with our longings, dreams, and passions. The brain will not dedicate energy to that intimacy if it thinks that it might be attacked, humiliated, or abandoned. This is why the first year is dedicated to establishing psychological ground, orientation, and resourcing. This means that you will learn how to feel safe in your body, alone and with others. I want you to have the experience of being together without experiencing anxiety or fear. This takes a lot of practice, time, and patience.

Do not rush through this task. It might seem boring and slow but think about what you are doing: Rewiring perceptions of sensory input and adjusting how your nervous system responds to real or imagined threats. You are trying to create a place of safety in an unsafe world. This place of safety allows for deeper states of regulation and this in turn allows for meaningful connections to emerge.

Safety is not just a concept. It should be explored throughout your different bodies. There are emotional, physical, mental, and soulful flavors to safety. Each demands a different approach.[38] For example, you might rationally know that you are safe while your body keeps sending signals that you are in danger.

Each level of the tribe will need different tools and practices to establish safety. There is personal safety, safety with others, and a general sense of safety in the tribe. When safety and grounding are not the highest priority in group work, attachment and trauma triggers may flare up. This can cause emotional turbulence in the group and it is probably one of the main reasons that people leave communities and relationships. For example, depression has been correlated to misinterpreting other people's facial expressions, and trauma to how a person perceives danger.

Perceiving a safe situation to be dangerous or experiencing somebody as angry when they are actually unaroused can be a hurdle for connection. Here are three potential outcomes of not putting enough emphasis on safety:

Avoiding drama: People with an avoidant attachment style, introverts, trauma survivors, and some personality types perceive conflict as unsafe and may sound the alarm. Difficult dynamics may trigger attachment wounds and past trauma. This can be overwhelming and some will quickly become fed up with all this 'drama.' They will then project, displace, blame, and hurt anyone who is believed to be a source of the dysregulation they are feeling. These individuals will be uninclined to work things out and the group might lose an important perspective.

Blaming others: It only takes a few members to derail and emotionally exhaust a group. For some, blame is the ammunition against vulnerability. For others, blame is a way to avoid taking responsibility for their life. Regardless, when people cannot contain their chaos and bring it into an already strenuous task of building relationships, people become hurt and scared. This can be especially confusing when dealing with undiagnosed borderline personality disorder or traits of sociopathy.

Isolating: When people and communities feel attacked, they may choose to isolate — passively or with active aggression — from the outside world. This reaction to a general sense of danger is specifically perilous because it prevents a much-needed reality check and dialogue among those who are not part of the community. Isolation can lead to arrested development of the community and reduced accountability of people's actions.

A truly safe space is an ever-deepening empathetic exchange that is not dominated by how things should be done. For example, if Jack is triggered by Jill, does that make Jill wrong? The answer is unclear until Jill and the other members support Jack to find the words and feelings to process and express his concerns, while Jill can still share her perspective.

So, once again, please keep the conversations relatively light for the first year and avoid unsolicited advice or feedback. Fuse this core need into whatever programs you are already running and try to include as many spiritual elements as possible as you design your year. Please remember that safety should not be considered a burden your community work. It is a basic yet critical task that can be implemented by adding already-established practices such as mindfulness, orientation, and grounding.

We are lucky to live in a time that there is so much awareness of the need for safety in group work. I encourage you to see the bibliography for resources or do your own extended research through online trainings, books and courses.

YEAR TWO: Needs | Sameness
Somatic Aliveness, permission to explore & the fulfilment of needs

- **Orient to now (play and pleasure)**
- **Measure of success:** A reduction in personal and collective shaming; Increased willingness to explore feelings, needs, and deep soul-requests.
- **Questions for group members to explore:** Do you feel more courageous? Are you willing to explore yourself (without shame)?
- **You are ready for the next year when...** People take more risks with themselves and others; they try out new behaviors, values, feelings; they have found their *yes* and their *no*.
- **Trouble spots:** There is radicalization in the group. This may include extreme behaviors, unhealthy risk-taking, too much change, members feeling overwhelmed, members saying yes to things they don't want to do in order to please the group; peer and group pressure.

◇◇◇◇◇◇◇◇◇◇◇◇

Year two is about giving oneself and others permission to explore individual and group edges without shame or fear. It is the lively search of the parts you might have lost as a child. Liberated from expectations, and the need to perform, this year focuses on playing rather than arriving. When you begin to give yourself permission to meet all of your needs, you will develop an intimate proximity with a range of emotions, needs, sensations, and perspectives; you will learn to speak honestly about your challenging and difficult experiences and re-connect to your life force.

I believe that spiritual approaches that also offer a healing space for the integration of the self are needed. This is the foundation (or ground) that allows the transpersonal Self to emerge, where one is truly connected to a deeper existential and contemplative life (Friedman, 1964), a life that is for self and others as well as for the planet at large.

Therefore, year two begins with the integration of shadow, through cognitive or behavior adjustment and the exploration of one's narratives and values. This can help members reach a certain level of clarity about their needs and how to express them, gain insight into their values and narrative, and reach a higher sense of wellbeing and self-love. It also supports the exploration of one's emotional life and of one's capacity to have healthy transactions with others and with oneself;

Eventually, this becomes the ground for the transpersonal, where through contemplative practices, an introduction to a wider map of the human psyche can support (or suggest) a higher potential for a deeper existential life, where the members recognize their unique self, and its' expression as a poetic life— endlessly expanding, evolving, and exploring the inner and outer domains of their existence.

The more intimate you become with aspects of yourself, the more you will be able to live a life that is free of shame. Life can then flow through you and you will learn to build confidence in your own humanity by being at one with your experiences, regardless of how painful, scary, or unpleasant they may be. Your comfort with a fuller range of feelings and your growing capacity to know and express your needs will yield further coherence and joy.

Each gesture toward play and pleasure should be nested within the grounded experience of safety you developed in year one. Practice this with yourself and respect the capacities of the diverse people that make up your tribe. Use the contemplative elements to stretch and expand, shifting slowly from what you already know to what is still to be known.

Because of the diverse nature of the community every member, group, and lineage will have a different relationship to the exploration of their edges. You want to be as conscious of this in your community as possible, because then the conversation shifts from how people *should be* exploring to where people are *really* at.

Which brings us to diversity: One of the most important aspects of the CODE is how it interprets diversity. Diversity in this respect is a virtue, and not an objective that needs to be achieved for its own sake. It is not an end, but a quality. In this sense, diversity is the (ongoing, alive) starting point for meaningful dialogue, not a goal in its own right. As we have seen in previous chapters, when we confuse a psychological force like diversity with a *worldview-based concept*, then love and curiosity are slowly replaced by shame, blame, and dogma; the shadow of diversity is the shaming of otherness. And when people are shamed into diversity submission for not conforming to a particular worldview, then ethnocentric worldviews are more likely to gain power around the globe. Fear of otherness can then be introduced appropriately and integrated slowly into the collective space. What matters most is not the level of openness a person or a group has, but the intention of the community to lean into shame-free curiosity.

This is the work you explore in year two if you wish to (re)enter the all-inclusive reality field, this great perfection that is life. It is a humbling exploration because you get to say *maybe* to perspectives that you are usually unwilling to engage with. You get to find nuggets of truth and falsehood at the core of every worldview, including those that you personally hold dear. This is how you will begin to be able to build bridges between what formerly seemed to be 'wrong' worldviews.

Most people have complex and nuanced ideas about immigration, civil rights, poverty, racism, income, abortion, and education. If you choose to stay open to the dialectical tension these issues provoke, the tribe will be able to see how all perspectives hold value. No one is completely wrong and no one is completely right. This, in turn, will teach you that each and every worldview is not only legitimate (when healthy) but has validity and importance to the health of the whole community.

YEAR THREE: Significance | Belonging
Will, power, autonomy & actualization

- **Orient to Self (Self actualizing)**
- **Measures of success:** Feeling good enough; Aligning with agency and personal power.
- **Questions for group members to explore:** Who would you be if you didn't have to impress anyone? Who would you be if you felt that you are *enough*? If you felt lovable?
- **You are ready for the next year when...** People have developed a healthy sense of self that is not shaped or defined by others. Boundaries mature, and people are better in touch with their needs; a clear value system that is independently yours emerges.
- **Trouble spots:** Rigidity, inflexibility, self-obsession, narcissism and egocentric behaviors.

Not much self-respect and weak boundaries?
No mature and healthy love!

◇◇◇◇◇◇◇◇◇◇◇◇

We all carry the wounds of childhood and the inter-generational traumas of our parents and ancestors. We want to please and belong. We fear ridicule and shame. In some cases, we still don't know what we stand for, what we need, and who we want to be when we grow up. Sometimes just exploring these things is painful and overwhelming. It can disorient and paralyze us or provoke a flood of grief, disappointment, and confusion that were buried deep inside.

One thing that can help is using the organizing principle of rhythm. Start with your animalistic body and build on that. Observe your sleeping, resting, playing, and eating habits. Discover what pleases your body and do that daily. Keep it simple with statements like *this feels pleasant and this does not*, and slowly increase the complexity of your practice.

You will learn to lean into yourself because there is a deep knowing inside of you. It will teach you what is right and what is wrong *for you*. You will slowly establish the capacity to connect and love yourself. If you will practice this on a daily basis, you *will* come alive to the life force that echoes in you through change, and slowly learn that you can stop manipulating yourself and others to get what you need. Instead, you will *ask* for what you need.

I think of the Book of Exodus in the Old Testament, where Moses struggles to raise his hands so the people of Israel will win the battle. When gravity pulls Moses's hands to the ground (representing fear) Israel loses, and when Moses lifts his hands (representing grace) Israel wins. To some extent, we are all like Moses confronting the gravitational force of our psychological drives such as survival, pleasure, belonging, self-esteem, and knowledge. The beauty and challenge is to become aware of our conditioning (gravity) while simultaneously seeing that conditioning as something we do not have to be bound by (grace).

Without a secure enough self, there is really no *other*. Love, relationships, and healthy communications flourish among two or more people who know their own power, value, and needs. Any other versions of love are usually some form of enmeshment and co-dependency. So, let me remind you once more—you are good enough! Not perfect, but good enough. Try to say "I am good enough" a few times and see how it feels.

> *You deserve to feel loved (yes, deserve).*
> *You are worthy of respect.*
> *You can ask for help.*
> *You can say 'no.'*
> *Free from the burdens that haunt you,*
> *you do not have to be more or do more.*

8 | PREPARATION: FROM ME TO WE (YEAR FOUR AND YEAR FIVE)

The tribe is entering the second stage of collaboration. If the first stage was focused on generating mutual respect and curiosity, then the second will be focused on developing higher levels of collaboration and a deeper experience of belonging. Think of years one to three as preparatory training for the harder, more complex work of connecting that is the focus of years four and five. In the first three years, you built a foundation upon which the efforts of the next phase will flourish.

Think of a house as a metaphor for what I just discussed: some of us may be so intrigued by the design of each room of the house (its unique color, the different shapes of the space, and what furnishings make the house functional and warm) that we may forget to pay attention to the foundation of the house—what keeps the house standing. We all agree that when designing a house, a proper foundation should be laid, but because we take the foundation, the land on which the house was built, and even the engineering skills needed *for granted*, we eventually forget about all those initial and critical matters and become transfixed on the interior design and living conditions.

The intention of the first three foundational years was to heal, learn, and grow. And now those skills will be called on as we dive deeper into the collective space. The first three tasks (safety, meeting our needs, and knowing our significance) will remain central to *every single collaborative moment* to come. In each and every developmental task, the emphasis is on reclaiming the community in (and as) God and its manifestation in your relationships and your day-to-day life.

By now, each and every lineage, group, and the tribe as a whole should have a good enough understanding of the basic tenets of the community. You and other members should feel safe *enough* in your bodies (physical, emotional-sensual, relational, cognitive, wisdom-essence, and spirit) and safe *enough* with each other.

This shift to collaborative spiritual work is what makes year four and five so exciting and difficult! Your individual journey, the wisdom of your lineages, the growing complexity and the diversity of your community are coming together. The group is beginning to co-create the mind of God. This is unprecedented, so you are bound to make mistakes. How can you not when you are on the road to an unknown destination? By now the members of your tribe will have developed the skill to communicate their needs, perspectives, and value systems. But striking a balance between perspectives and finding a common ground between groups and lineages may still appear challenging.

How do you move together when everybody's point of view is right?

How do you shift from maintaining mutual respect into developing a shared, synergetic vision?

Years four and five might be somewhat hellish — but it is what you, as a community, will need for the emergence of a new collective. Building long term relationships is hard work! More complexity means more friction, which means more generated heat. So, I want you to think of the CODE as a cooling system that allows your collaborative adventures to work without overheating. You will rub each other the wrong way, evoke strong emotions, negotiate power dynamics, and act in manipulative, ignorant, and unkind ways.

The magic of collective resistance. I am going to assume that some members of your tribe will not be interested in moving forward with the tasks of year four and five. This may manifest consciously or as passive resistance. This resistance will come both from established religious groups in the community and from people who subscribe to more pluralistic worldviews. Here's why: It is tough to give up the journey of personal growth (both psychologically and spiritually), and it is especially challenging to give it up for demanding, long-term, psycho-spiritual, relational work. It is one thing to experience bliss with strangers during a retreat, or to absorb a psychological workshop over a weekend. It's a whole different story when you do that same kind of deep personal work for a long time with a group of people who see the world differently from you. The work of year four and five can seem laborious and exhausting, and may well stir up vulnerability.

Long-term spiritual, collaborative and developmental work that includes different lineages and developmental stages is not only rare, but also full of potential pitfalls. The deepening of love and vulnerability might trigger early attachment wounding. Becoming overwhelmed or ashamed as a result of hitherto unprocessed longings and grief might become common.

As such, I urge you to undertake the work of years four and five as slowly as you can. Remember what you are actually trying to deal with a level of complexity that humans have never faced before without escaping, distorting, blaming, minimizing, spiritually bypassing, or shaming. Have regular attachment ceremonies to meet the psycho-social needs of your members, so that everyone can feel secure with the others in the group.

YEAR FOUR: Love | Independence
Connection, love, & healthy relationships

- ꙮ **Orient to love (Connect)**
- ꙮ **Measures of success:** Willingness to depend on each other; people feel that they matter.
- ꙮ **Questions for group members to explore:** Do I belong to this place? Can I speak my truth and stay connected? Do I matter? What is my place in this community? If I leave, how will people react? What does it mean to be together?
- ꙮ **You are ready for the next year when...** The community feels a deep sense of connection—this may be stronger in the lineages and weaker in the tribe. Belonging is an internal experience, but it needs others to be felt.
- ꙮ **Trouble spots:** People might feel too exposed or unsafe; triggering of attachment wounds; deterioration of the community; groups might start to isolate and/or split.

◇◇◇◇◇◇◇◇◇◇◇◇◇

Year four will involve some form of reckoning. This is a healthy sign of the maturation of love in your community. It means that your members have established robust levels of individuation and boundaries (reckoning does not happen in cults where neither individuation nor boundaries are developed!). You will learn how to balance your humanity with your divinity, while still maintaining the complexity and diversity present in your community.

This is the year that you will make the leap into the transpersonal. You will notice a shift from personal work into the collective domain for which you have been laying the foundation over the past three years. This is where personal stories are transcended (not abandoned!) to include the tribe at large.

A triple sense of belonging will become established: to the self, to the lineage, and to the tribe. You will feel reunited with your ecological home, the world soul, and divine spirit. In this transformation, ownership and responsibility are understood as love. Each person matters, each perspective makes a difference, and you can live in many worlds at the same time.

Think of year four as a practicum in love. This is a dialogue with love about love to create love. You will grow comfortable with the paradox of love and curious about what else can be loved. Now, it is impossible to know how each of you will manifest your own unique expression of love. Instead I chose to use the organizing principle of the CODE to outline some possible landmarks for this task/year:

Holonism: You will discover new layers of love in yourself, in relationships, and as a community. You will come to know firsthand that love has an (unknown?) course and that it is an alive force that expands and contracts, flourishes and dies. As such, it is critical that you do not lose yourself in others, and that you do not sacrifice one good enough connection for a new shiny one. This is why boundaries are so important.

What may feel like a whole package of love and connection is *always* part of something bigger. The tribe is designed to be a structure within a structure (within a structure...), so if and when things fall apart on one level, you can still belong on another. Beware of statements like, "This is the *only* place where I can be myself/feel safe/learn about love/ speak my truth..."; "I found myself here"; "I am just so happy. I didn't think this kind of joy was possible!". These are warning signs. They have little to do with love. Your community is not special. Your teachers are not awake. You are whole on your own. You are whole in your relationships. But you and your community are never complete.

Balance: If the community has done enough personal work, the experience in year four will be rich and deep. Nevertheless, there are a few balancing acts that the community will negotiate in year four, including: loving self versus loving others, connecting with your own lineage versus connecting with other lineages, and the time invested in oneself versus the time invested in the community. On one extreme, the tribe might deepen its isolation. This may occur due to poor leadership that encourages supremacy ("We are so special…," and so on). On the other extreme, the group might find itself unable to sustain the deepening of vulnerability and connection, which may result in fragmentation, tension, and resentment.

Creativity: Connection feels good—so good that people are willing to do stupid, dangerous, and selfish things to feel it. Learning about love and connection is going to blow people's minds. They are going to taste new flavors of love, and this is the point of year four. But you will also meet the chaos and messiness that comes along with love and connection. You will encounter how difficult it is to control or manage love, why love hurts, and why you sometimes inadvertently act to avoid it.

Rhythm: Every person has their own rhythms of love, connection, and letting go. Some of these rhythms are borrowed and old. They are foreign to your heart and bring pain to your soul. Year four offers an opportunity to discern the organic from the unnatural. You are encouraged to let go of your social expectations so that you can find your innate rhythms. Then, and only then, will you come back to teach the beat that only you can drum.

Presence: Because year four involves so much risk-taking, it is important to lean into the embrace of our natural perfection, where all is already complete, healed, and connected. Year four is dedicated to awakening to your interdependency with the natural world, life, and God as community—endlessly expanding, exploring, and evolving the inner and outer domains. Aware of the inescapable, life-giving, and interwoven connections (that already are *you*), you will find your place in the world as a distinctive embodiment of life. This sense of belonging and connection will support the blossoming of a strong experiential awareness of your life force and its value, as well as your impact on and importance to others. You will also slowly develop the ability to express and communicate with greater honesty, integrity, and vulnerability.

YEAR FIVE: Being Known | Communication
Life as art. Expression & communication.

 Orient to communication (Differentiating)

 Measures of success: Subtler and more mature skills of communication.

 Questions for group members to explore: Can I listen? What does it mean to be honest? Can I be radically honest? Can I speak my truth while being present with you? Can I be empathetic?

 You are ready for the next year when... People know how to ask for what they want while caring for others; people's empathy is growing; people have been truthful and honest with each other and still want to come back to meetings; people are excited about being part of the community.

 Trouble spots: People feeling hurt, betrayed, unseen, or overwhelmed by unskillful honesty.

◇◇◇◇◇◇◇◇◇◇◇◇

Year five is an invitation to embrace your relational nature. It is an even deeper dive into the relational field to self, others, and God. Empathy, care, and curiosity have been cultivated for the past four years and the community can easily access these tools for dialogue. Being seen and feeling a sense of belonging is no longer a peak experience —

it is the new baseline for the community.

Year five demands the cultivation of communication tools that is simple and practical but also sacred—*the willingness and capacity to listen*. As this capacity grows, you begin to master the art of emptying yourself to make room for the intelligence of silence. The *space between* becomes the leader. The dialogue *is* the change. The presence of simply being accommodates diverse perspectives in a relational awareness that does not sacrifice the self.

Every single person has the responsibility for this quality of communication. You will shift from the center to the periphery (and back to the center) with ease, as you will come to notice what you can and cannot bring to the *space between* in any given moment. It will become noticeable (and thus manageable) when the group is overwhelmed or when someone is hijacking a meeting. Leadership then becomes transformative, flexible, and intuitive.

Each expression will find its place, allowing the unfolding nature of God to be seen by itself from a diversity of perspectives. Each point of view will be valued and settled in a natural dynamic hierarchy of ideas. And from this place, more and more will be acknowledged, felt, and known. Through this kind of dialogue, members will experience moments when the barriers between worldviews and perspectives dissolve and new integrative wisdom is born.

The shift from individuals speaking in a circle to relational engagement and eventually to transformative dialogue marks the evolution of the impulse (as it appears in your community)—spontaneously arising in real time to mend fragmentation. Even when the environment is scary and emotionally charged, new relational possibilities will be co-created on the altar of radical listening, in the space between answers, ideas, fears, and opinions.

9 | TAKEOFF: INSIGHTS AND FRUITION (YEAR SIX AND SEVEN)

Y ou have now been together for five years! Some members have left and new members have joined. The challenges of year four and five are slowly giving way to personal and collective rhythms that function as a harmonious pulse (for most people). You feel more comfortable with ambiguity and can hold a balance between your own needs, the needs of the community, and the demands of your lineages you belong to.

There is the ripening of self-love, self-acceptance, and the embodied experience of safety. Many have had powerful experiences, including resting in the ease of their own being. They sense either more connected to their authentic spiritual tradition or have found lineages and groups where they feel at home. Ceremonies, rituals, traditions, stories, little sayings and jokes, regrets and missed opportunities have mixed together to create a glue that bond you.

Any *projected* ideas about what this may look like before this stage are most likely the old disguised as the new. I do not assume to know what these collaborative experiments will look like. I can share, however, what I imagine years six and seven may feel like.

The tribe, as a whole, should feel somewhat established before moving ahead to the tasks of years six and seven. You have been striving to adapt and evolve since year one. Even though your vision has been present since the beginning, until now you have been focused on personal and relational work. But without the completion of that groundwork, there can be no takeoff.

Things should get really interesting in years six and seven! The relational property ushers in the discovery of new insights. Curiosities will transform into solutions. Change will feel palpable. This is not only about emerging insights on a group level, but also your growing ability to pendulate between different psycho-spiritual developmental levels and hierarchical perspectives.

Through this amazing process, your personal and collective inner world will evolve into something that none of us can imagine today. This will be the ripening of your cooperative journey. In the hallway of a thousand doors (the collective mind) the fog of your worldview will give way to untapped possibilities. With time and patience, your capacity to observe and then impact the community you have worked to build will bring new applied insights. Emerging from the pressure cooker of the process, your embodied, participatory insights will forge new, interconnected pathways that need to be explored. Each and every tribe will map a distinctive collaborative journey — in an endless variations of the body of God.

YEAR SIX: Vision | Action
Mastering value-based commitment to action.

- **Orient to vision and action**

- **Measures of success:** The vision is oriented toward the developmental emergence of the impulse as it manifests distinctly in each and every tribe.

- **Questions for group members to explore:** Who are we as a group? What is our common vision as a micro-religion? What happened to us over the past five years?

- **You are ready for the next year when...** The vision can hold lineages together, new insights and breakthroughs become common, and a collaborative action is established.

- **Trouble spots:** Intellectualization, the pull and push of the different groups, the inability to transcend and include something new. People might feel excluded; groups might try to simplify things.

◇◇◇◇◇◇◇◇◇◇◇◇◇

How will you serve the impulse in your own way?

What is your version of collaborative spirituality?

What do want to give to the world?

What have you learned that you think is important to share?

These are some of the questions that you will try to

answer in year six. Your growing ability to feel safe, play, deepen connections, and improve communication will help you to explore them.

Any insight that will be born in year six belongs to you. I don't mean belong in a corporate trademark fashion. Your tribe has worked together for more than five years and by now has the psycho-spiritual capacity to share any insight that has arisen, and to create new structures to address the many challenges we are facing in the world today.

In this respect, year six differs because of the level of ownership of the future. It sparks grounded enthusiasm that brings forth new structures and practical ideas within the religious context to solve what currently seems unsolvable. Due to the nature of the process, the solutions and new structures will be flexible enough to translate their meaning to different worldviews and incorporate simple enough solutions that can then be distributed.

A word of caution for year six: Many collectives tend to default into repeating what has been done in the past—what seems like a new idea may be an old idea in new clothes.[38] This does not mean that you should throw away tradition, knowledge, and past wisdom. The CODE is not about getting rid of what you know or who you are. Rather, it focuses on integrating each and every worldview into a bigger, more inclusive vision. Krishnamurti (1946) writes:

The observer and the observed are one; the thinker and his thoughts are one. To experience the thinker and his thought as one is very arduous for the thinker is ever taking shelter behind his thought; he separates himself from his thoughts to safeguard himself, to give himself continuity, permanency; he modifies or changes his thoughts, but he remains (para 8)

As mentioned before, if it feels like something you and others have done in the past five years, it's not the future. After all, you are your past— your experiences, history, culture, pain and memories. Your past is the source of all of the psychological forces that allowed you to create this new vision for yourself. And thus, only through the acknowledgment of who you are (as the past), you have the possibility to leap into the unknown.

YEAR SEVEN: Wholeness | Duality
Mastering union and fruition (Execution).

- ◈ **Orient to awareness-integration (harvesting).**
- ◈ **Measures of success:** The group has integrated new insights about its collaborative spiritual work.
- ◈ **Questions for group members to explore:** Does the process feel alive? Is the tribe living its common vision—as a community and as individuals? Does the process feel alive?
- ◈ **You are ready for the next year when...** There is a sense of maturation and ease; people are now shifting into mentoring roles and are starting their own tribes.
- ◈ **Trouble spots:** Grief and loss; unwillingness to let go; concerns around the leadership team; people don't want the leadership to change; collapse of the tribe.

◇◇◇◇◇◇◇◇◇◇◇◇

You made it to year seven! If the tribe is still together, then the vision that was created in year six will now have a year to be executed. The vision will be nested within all of the developmental tasks that came before it. It has matured to influence all of the dimensions of your life and it has had a practical and significant impact on people's lives. A steady aliveness flows through the vessel your tribe has created.

The process has supported the tribe to hold a growing diversity of perspectives. The tribe became a collective pool of creativity for socio-cultural solutions.

Think of year seven as the year you get to juggle *all* of the developmental balls you have worked with until now. These will be heightened moments when the future can be felt. This idea is the heart of the CODE and what I believe the impulse is asking us (itself, don't forget!) to *do* and *be*.

For me, year seven is the real mystery. It is a sacred time for your tribe. I ask that you enter it with as few preconceived notions of what it will entail as possible. Set this as an intention and do your best to be open. It is so easy to project a spiritual ending and then live that imagined perception instead of being present to the emerging movement. It is even more difficult when you are involving other people, because more people mean a higher likelihood of misunderstandings.

Remember that you can always lean back on the other tasks, the organizing principles, and the elements for guidance in those moments. You can slow or completely stop the process until you and others are back in your psychological and spiritual capacity.

Art-based projects can provide a container to process all that happens in and to you and the tribe at large. From exhibitions to publications to concerts and multimedia performances, the use of art will support the digestion and integration of insights that have arisen and your ability to share with the world.

Again, *try not to rush*. It might feel easier to wrap it all up with a nice bow and declare that you have arrived. You have not arrived. You never will. So, stay with the insights, keep on integrating them in your community and family life, and into the work you do in the world. Practice juggling—try to keep all of the developmental tasks and principles you have come to know intimately in the past years in the air at once. Watch them fall in front of you and then pick them up again, and again. Juggle with friends, other members, at work. Let the juggling penetrate your dreams and your day-to-day activities.

Year seven is a year of endings and new beginnings because you are preparing yourself to start a new cycle. Some members will be leaving, either to start their own communities or because they received what they needed and are done. The leadership is also transitioning—training a new team to take their place for the next cycle of the CODE.

The new leadership might shadow the old team for the first year, but eventually they must take their place. This exchange, theoretically, will happen six more times (a maximum of 49 years) until the community dissipates. I say dissipate because I believe that no matter how successful a spiritual community is, it should restructure after seven years and end at some point… And around and around it will go.

You are a new spark of the impulse. And if all goes well, an orientation toward inter-subjective relationships will occur and a paradoxical realization will take place where you will see that the one *is* many and yet, no other is present. All of your worldviews and perspectives and your sense of self will become fluid and you will shift with ease from self-centric to group-centric to world-centric points of view.

Let it be a celebration! Enjoy the deepening of your friendships and reflect on the journey you have taken, on how you have changed, and on what you have learned. Honor where you have been and the courage it took to risk it all. Listen to the impulse that has asked you to walk to a new promised land. If you are willing to remain vulnerable and curious, and to take responsibility for your life force, then you will be rewarded not only through having better experiences, but by taking your place as a co-evolutionary partner with divinity.

10 | RED FLAGS: LEARNING FROM MISTAKES

I am passionate about group processes. I am a strong believer in the power of groups to transform people. I have seen this happen in the groups I have been facilitating for more than 20 years. There is something special about group work that I don't think can be replicated through personal work. The transformational power of relational work comes from the presence of diverse peer perspectives, transference, mirroring, and feedback.

However (and this is a big however), one must stay aware of the dangers always lurking in group work, especially in the domains of spirituality and psychology. These types of inner-work groups are adventurous and exploratory and, unchecked, they can become emotionally and psychologically dangerous.

If we are to serve the emerging call for collaboration,

then our *yes* must be discerning and cautious. One of my most beloved Buddhist teachers, Lama Mark Webber, often says that the heart needs to cultivate discernment and right intent. You have freedom to say yes, to taking emotional risks, to experimentation with ideas—but is it always right? Good? Beneficial? True to your values and culture? How do you know?

In the second episode of the Canadian Broadcasting Corporation's 2019 podcast series, "Escaping NXIVM," they describe a situation where a group of women were asked to sear a symbol onto their upper hips as initiation to a secret women's-only group. One of the women who participated told the CBC that they were asked to repeatedly say, "Master, please brand me, it would be an honor," while a NXIVM-affiliated physician performed the pain-inducing act. The woman had doubts. She wanted to scream and run away, but she did not. She chose to do something to her body which was against her values and common sense. She bought in to the story that the initiation was an act of loyalty and a sign of her commitment to personal growth.

You might ask, how could a successful, intelligent, educated woman allow herself to participate in such a painful and humiliating ritual? Why are people willing to hurt themselves, hurt others, or even die for their group—be it a cult, religious organization, or government?

The brilliant Netflix documentary series "Wild, Wild, Country," about Bhagwan Shree Rajneesh (Osho), his assistant Ma Anand Sheela, and their followers, presents another example of what can go wrong with even the best of intentions. Rajneesh, a controversial teacher and "God-man," was teaching a radical form of meditation and philosophy in an effort to bridge Eastern and Western philosophy. In the second chapter, we see Sheela speaking about the community they formed as a kind of "heaven on earth," while residents of the nearest town perceive the community as invaders.

By episode three, Sheela and other leaders, who are supposed to be following Rajneesh's teaching of mindfulness, love, creativity, and humor, are teaching community members to use semi-automatic rifles. In episode four, we see the community in full confrontation with the local town and county for what can only be described as a hostile takeover of one culture by another. By episode five, Sheela and other members are actively plotting to assassinate a local official and the personal doctor of Rajneesh. The community eventually is closed after Rajneesh escapes and is later captured by immigration officers, and Sheela serves time for her crimes.

How is it possible that a guru who teaches love and mindfulness would allow his community to deteriorate into using controlling, greedy, and terrorizing tactics to gain power? A cynic might say this is the nature of human beings. A more conservative person might take what happened as an example of moral deterioration. What happened could also be understood as the outcome of indoctrination. But how would that be possible if the purpose of Rajneesh's teachings was to celebrate individuation and to free people from the bonds of their cultures of origin? Did the members of the community not see the paradox? Was Rajneesh not aware of what Sheela and his closest students were doing? Is this the fate of any group seeking to live an alternative life separated from mainstream culture?

Rajneesh's social experiment was not the first or the last to show great promise at the outset, only to end painfully (traumatically, even) for its members. The list is long and ranges from extreme and tragic endings (e.g., Heaven's Gate, the Branch Davidians, and The People's Temple, to name a few), to more mild endings (e.g., Buddhafield, the Children of God, and The Source Family). What has gone wrong and why does this keep happening to so many intentional communities seeking to advance culture? And why has this been occurring throughout history, even in all major religions?

There are many reasons why these communities eventually dissolved. However, for the purposes of this book, I would like to highlight stories that offer lessons to those who wish to build a community with religious or spiritual intentions. To do so, I will use one of the five principles of the CODE as my guide.

Each of the communities I mentioned lacked humanity and did not pay attention to the developmental tasks of their members. To some extent, this is an unfair criticism because it is the very nature of an operating system not to see its own limitations until it is time to adapt due to changing circumstances. In the case of Rajneesh's community (and

I am only speaking about the Rajneeshpuram experiment in this context), Sheela and the inner circle embodied an egocentric and power-driven stage of development when the county started to push back against their vision.

From that moment forward, the community's advanced values were dominated by a baser defensive impulse. This was demonstrated by weaponizing the city, by the assassination attempts, by secretly recording other members, by power moves against members of the community and the neighboring town, and by disregard for people who did not share the same value systems.

If you watched the documentary series, you might remember how slowly but surely some leading members of the community enforced their resolve with little or no resistance. The community they invaded had a level of maturation that their supposedly more advanced, progressive group did not possess.

The depth of disrespect and contempt harbored by the community members is evident from the documentary. Scant care was expressed for what was happening to anybody who lived in the town. This suggests that the process of individuation was not mature in the community. If it had been, people would have been allowed to explore and voice their concerns, challenge the teacher and the leadership team, and maintain clear boundaries.

True, there was a lot of freedom to explore spirituality and sexuality. The members experimented and challenged the dominant cultural norms of their time, but their motivations seemed to come from egocentrism. There was a strong emphasis on radical liberation, where *everything* was allowed. Very little consideration was expressed for anything or anybody outside of or at the fringe of the group.

I would like you to notice what happens when this kind of worldview is not integrated with other, *as important*, personal needs and collective outlooks. A more developed version of that community would have considered the perspectives and concerns of the people who lived in the neighboring town. They would have respectfully engaged in dialogue, and members would have comfortably critiqued the behavior of their leaders. What we can learn from this case is that communities and groups are always at risk of devolving to this level of behavior when threatened or when there is not enough understanding of how to integrate their egocentric (and group-centric) needs with those of a larger context.

THE POWER OF GROUPS

It is easy to dismiss the power of a group by saying that only weak people join cults or act against their will. That is just not true. Most people join groups because they want to make their lives and the lives of others better. Most of the people who join these types of groups have good intentions. However, utopian visions often give way to dystopian realties in the shadow of manipulative leadership and unquestionable ideologies.

We are all capable of being influenced to perform unsafe and uncomfortable actions to ourselves and others. We can find ourselves unwittingly embracing a group mentality that pushes people past their comfort and safety thresholds. It is true that young adults are more at risk, but we are all capable of doing terrible things with enough indoctrination and manipulation. If you need more proof, Google "the Stanford prison experiment," or listen to interviews with people who left intentional communities.

I have identified seven major concerns that can jeopardize the integrity of groups. None of these concerns are new, but they are more likely to present themselves in complex processes like the CODE:

Groups can be a powerful aphrodisiac. Groups can be influential, seductive, and manipulative. This is not only the case when they are fronted by a charismatic leader. The group as an entity can attract people with promises of belonging, a vision of hope to ease, heal, or make better our wounds and pain. And sometimes, for some people, they do! People do report feelings of increased belonging, a renewed trust in their ability to make a difference, a clear psycho-spiritual map of how the world works. This is what Giddens (1991) termed "ontological security"—a stable mental state that comes from a sense of continuity in one's mind. By reinforcing ideas through proximity (reading the same books, adhering to the same values and ideas), groups can become dangerous to their members and in extreme situations to others. In return for ontological security, some people are willing to sacrifice choice, critical thinking, and personal power or agency. This does not mean that group work cannot transform a person, but there is a real danger of overriding a person's will, especially in cases where weakened boundaries are already present.

Human development: People are complicated and ambiguous. They bring their histories of pain, disappointment, and maladaptive behaviors into their present relationships. They also often have attachment styles that make communication and commitment difficult. And of course, each individual sees, hears, and perceives reality differently. What is scary for one can be enjoyable for another. Something perceived as a threat by one might be experienced as boundary-setting by another. When people try to work toward a goal in a community setting, situations will at times almost certainly become weird, confusing, and overwhelming. There will be projection, strained relational dynamics, and other threats that need to be taken into consideration. This is one of the reasons that the CODE was designed as an intentionally slow process focused as much on human development, and why year one specifically is dedicated to laying the foundations of group safety. Attending to staged developmental needs in a manner that is not rushed will prepare the group to address inevitably challenging issues that will crop up with time.

Shadow: In 2011, the Vancouver Canucks lost game seven of the Stanley Cup Finals. At the time, my wife and I were living very close to the arena where the game was held. I will never forget how our peaceful downtown neighborhood suddenly became a war zone. I remember encountering bleeding faces and bicycles being thrown into the air while out on a walk that afternoon. I immediately went back to our apartment and told my wife to turn on the news. It seemed like everybody in the streets that day had lost their minds! My wife and I followed the news that evening, watching in amazement how the windows of some of the more iconic buildings of downtown Vancouver were smashed. People set fire to cars and started fights with the police. My wife and I discussed how this was the perfect example of how the collective shadow is always just an inch under the surface of civilization. When it comes to the collective unconscious, shadow can be understood as the unwillingness of groups to deal with a collective blindness to their violence, brutality, and wickedness, and to address their past misdoings.

Getting lost in translation: Opportunities for misunderstanding, for words and emotions becoming lost in translation, are much higher in intentionally diverse groups than in more homogeneous groups. Indeed, any group that journeys into the uncharted territories of what is to come will experience growing pains that have to do with misunderstandings. This will inevitably push people's buttons. The intentionally slow pace and unique structure of the CODE can act as a buffer against this issue.

Isolation: Group isolation is among the biggest dangers of collective spirituality. It is amazing how many well-intended groups wind up becoming isolated. This results in less self-reflection, more fear of criticism, and a group-centric mentality (us versus them). Isolation happens so slowly that most groups in their early stages are unaware that it is even happening. By the time a community is isolated, it is usually too late for repair. Those who are still clear-minded and can think independently tend to leave and the remaining members usually see their departure as a sign that they must isolate even more to protect themselves. Group mentality is so powerful that even well-aware, mature individuals can fall under the spell of ideologies that promise salvation or solutions. Even good ideas can lead groups to do horrible things. Yes, even the ideas presented in this book! Without protective measures, most groups are doomed to follow this route. Being aware of these tendencies is one of the most important safeguards against the group enmeshment and the isolation of your group from mainstream society. This is why boundaries are so critical in group processes, and especially for religious or spiritual groups where notions of transcendence and enlightenment can be used in maladaptive ways to override personal needs.

Discernment and intent: Lacking discernment on the
personal or collective level means group members can
be badly hurt and can cause healthy communities to
fall apart. How can one know what is right and wrong?
What happens if someone challenges your hesitation
by saying that you are not committed to your personal
growth, or to God? How do you know when acting is
the right thing to do and when it might be harmful?
These are not just theoretical questions. They happen
all the time in day-to-day life. Should you stay in your
job? In a challenging relationship? Should you stay in
an organization that benefits you personally (and maybe
financially), but which hurts other members of your town
or the environment? Should you confront a spiritual
teacher who is wise most days but sometimes becomes
aggressive, immature, or disrespectful?

In discussing the importance of discernment, Lama
Mark Webber uses the simple example of an apple: you
can make a distinction between a ripe, juicy apple and a
rotting one. Why? Because you can feel it and because
you were trained. That is to say, you need to combine your
"Spidey senses" with additional training in observation
and by learning from past mistakes. There will usually
be signs, gut feelings, intuitions, and concerns that, when
ignored, may lead to unnecessary pain and sometimes
trauma. Learn and practice saying, "I am not okay with
this" or "I am a bit worried about what we are doing" and

stick to it until you feel that it is met with open curiosity and willingness to engage. It takes courage, no doubt, but also a lot of training to grow your inner permission to speak out. "You need to be more committed to the path" is not only a malicious statement but also a slippery slope into dangerous psychological territory. Spirituality is not a race, so take as much time as you need to grow familiar with your needs, values, and intentions.

Endings: Through my research, I have learned that most of the corruption, dysregulation, and bizarre behaviors in communities come to full formation after about eight to ten years. Therefore, I recommend that communities stop for (Self) evaluation after the seventh year of the CODE. Let that process die, change leadership, and then continue afresh if warranted and desired. Like anything organic, all authentic spiritual endeavors must eventually come to an end. When communities refuse the healthy process of ending or recycling themselves, the resulting stagnation can become toxic. Even well-intentioned people can become corrupted by power as leaders and with each passing year the likelihood of corruption grows substantially. This is true for individuals and it is true for religious organizations. Things need to end to make room for something new — be it a new leadership group or new ideas and views on religion and spirituality.

WHAT CAN BE DONE?

The good news is that most people *do not* join extreme groups or religious organizations specifically because of the above concerns. They have seen the misdeeds of cult leaders and group members so many times that they do not want to become the next victim or perpetrator. The not-so-good news is that our need to belong to something larger than ourselves is being ignored or cautiously sidestepped as a result of these kinds of stories

Can authentic collaborative spiritual work happen without these familiar looming shadows? Is this evil mandatory? Must all groups go through these issues or are there ways to prevent them? How can people become aware of maladaptive and destructive behaviors before they put the group at risk? And, are there ways to keep the tension between the personal and collective journey healthy? If spiritual belonging is a core human need, how can we better protect against these common risks?

Start with safety.
Lots of it.
Build trust.
Slowly.
And keep it small.
No grandiose visions.
No big promises.

Future communities will need to learn how to be discerning, stay open to new ideas, be flexible and willing (as opposed to rigid, scared, contracted). **How?** (1) By maintaining a clear personal value system. Take the time to figure this out for each and every member of the community; (2) having ethical guidelines for the community; (3) practicing the five principles; (4) leaning on the wisdom of the great traditions; (5) having a large and diverse leadership team that represents each and every lineage and group in the community; (6) adding processes that help your tribe maintain integrity and high ethical standards (not a general ethical standard, but one that comes from the community for the community); (7) remaining vigilant! Remember that each and every one of these pointers can be manipulated to work against you and your community. Actively learn about the mistakes of other groups—watch movies, read books, share stories.

WORKING WITH MENTAL HEALTH AND TRAUMA

We are who we are, and who we are is strange, unpredictable, and beautiful. Maybe we are all a bit depressed, all a bit mad. Maybe that's what "normal" really is. Maybe we need to acknowledge it all in order to grow into our own normality? Our symptoms are threads that can lead us to happiness, to an existence that we cannot otherwise imagine. Symptoms

RED FLAGS: LEARNING FROM MISTAKES

can be seen as a call to pay attention rather than to seek psychological or psychotropic treatment.

It is true that people feel better when they accept that they belong and are loved. It is also true that many psychological issues can be supported and sometimes healed through spiritual efforts, such as yoga and meditation. However, spiritual and religious communities sometimes become powerful tools for avoiding psychological issues. Spiritual bypassing can be irresponsible and dangerous. It occurs when someone uses spiritual concepts to avoid dealing with life. It can affect relationships, mental health, work, and perception of oneself.

One of my former clients used postural yoga to avoid feeling her grief and the deep sense of alienation she was experiencing. Another client described how he was trying to meditate to make his depression go away. In both cases, they could only heal when they were willing to challenge their belief systems and own their rage and grief.

These are just two examples out of numerous individuals with whom I worked where spiritual practices were used to either manipulate the self, or control situations and relationships that produced anxiety, fear, anger, or grief. Spiritual bypassing is more common among novice practitioners but can stick for a long time if not challenged.

So, let me put out a hard warning about mental health and trauma in communities:

First, the CODE is not a substitute for psychological treatment or medication when these are needed. This choice should be left to the individual and their family. There will be some community members who will have mental health issues. Some may choose to discontinue use of their medication because they believe this will help them to feel better in the community. This can cause symptoms that may be confusing, scary, or even dangerous, to reappear. As a psychotherapist who works with addiction, trauma, and depression, I have witnessed this firsthand many times and can testify that it is difficult to navigate when it happens.

Second, members might feel the pressure to discontinue their medication in communities where some members encourage them to do so. The assumption may be that they do not need those "toxic" drugs if they just do group work, therapy, start a new cleansing or detox diet, and so on. I wish mental health was so simple. People should be allowed to make choices for themselves without pressure. They should not feel that they are not being spiritual enough because they are taking medication or because they are scared to admit they are on medication.

Third, with the growing trend of using mind-altering substances like mushrooms, ayahuasca, and cannabis, it is important to note that these powerful substances *can* trigger mental health symptoms. It is rare, but it does happen. The risk of this is higher for young adults.

Fourth, the CODE is a multidisciplinary model that supports personal and group therapy. Please remember that therapy brings with it issues of trust, projection, and confusion of roles and therefore should be facilitated by non-members. Please draw on your ethical guidelines and psychological or counselling association for additional support.

Lastly, a word on trauma and post-traumatic stress disorder (PTSD). It is impossible to do developmental work or any meaningful psychospiritual work without at some point encountering trauma and associated mental health issues. Trauma is part of life and, until very recently, it was barely addressed, often ignored. I write this because bad things can happen to people and communities who do not put guidelines and protocols in place and draw on support from qualified therapists when working with trauma. So, get the professional help you need for your members and for the community at large.

I teach courses at a university on trauma and can tell you that it is a complex issue. I encourage both the leaders and members of the community to be as trauma-informed as possible. I have added a few resources on trauma in the reference list. There are also hundreds of therapeutic models that the community can learn from (e.g., humanistic, cognitive-behavioral, postmodern, family systems, acceptance-based, and spiritual). Most of them work well together and are complementary to spiritual work. I encourage each tribe, lineage, group, family and individuals to find the models that work for them.

And remember, the general rule of thumb in therapy is more on practicing empathy and listening and less on advice giving. Or, as Brené Brown says, "empathy, not sympathy" is key to change. People are going to be at different stages of readiness for change and it is important to meet them where they are, not where we think they *should* be.

11 | FINAL THOUGHTS

*Science teaches us that life needs
conditions for biological evolution
to happen. Religion offers relational
structures to spiritually to thrive.
But what does God teach us?*

In his song "Stone Soup," singer-songwriter Tom Chapin puts an old folktale to music. It is about a stranger who comes to a new town and makes a stone soup. As he makes the soup, eliciting help from all of the townspeople, he teaches them a lesson about sharing and cooperation. In Tom's version, the stranger is a soldier coming back from war. He is tired from his struggles and wants to be nourished. Despite the war, the soldier is playful, like the Fool in tarot cards—optimistic and carefree. No one gives him food or shelter. They all claim they have nothing to share. Instead of leaving in search of a new village, he drums his drum and declares that he is going to make a soup from a stone.

The village children become intrigued and hurry over to see what he is doing. They are curious about and less fearful of the stranger. He asks the children to add a stone, and then assures them, "This is gonna be good." The excited children want to try the soup, but the soldier tells them it is not ready. He asks each of the children to contribute one vegetable from each of their homes. With each new vegetable added, the scent grows more appetizing and eventually the adults start to come. In the end, everyone shares a beautiful "stone soup."

I love telling this story to my children because it speaks to the human capacity to overcome fear and to cooperate. In the story, the soldier—the misfit in town—is not manipulating the children but uses the skillful means of a master who knows how to work with fear and mistrust. He wants everybody to be included so he builds trust slowly, working first with only those who are willing. The soldier sees his need *and* the need of the whole village to be nourished. He understands that only through collaboration will all of them attain that goal. This is a powerful tale because it represents, archetypally, three aspects of the human psyche:

The soldier is the world soul. Behind him are the battles of past (past lives, or collective intergenerational pain). He can only be nourished with people and by people, in community. He uses a drum—his rhythmic beat attracts those who can still hear the call to participate in life, beyond fear. The call of the drum begs others to participate in unique ways, and also to meet in the *center* of the village. It is a call to believe in the unbelievable using creativity, play, and the power of collaboration.

The children represent the innocence of the psyche: Open mindedness, willingness, naivety, and the part of us that says yes to the soul's request to come together. In the song, the children do not have food with them to share. They have to go back home to get food to contribute. The homes have food, but the adults are unwilling to share. So, the children become the bridge. They are the trusting part of us that brings what is nourishing to the psyche (represented in the story as food). The children are the part of us that wants more connection. Not just in our traditional home, but in the collective space of the village. The children are willing to take that risk, to believe.

The adults are the part of the psyche that rejects or is afraid of the journey of the soul. The collective space is broken by the wars of past and the ego is tired of trying to connect. Each adult (or each tradition) does not want to share and is fearful of the unknown and mysterious.

The soldier is making soup out of a stone!
The adults do not believe that this is possible.
The children believe it is.

The stone he chooses has no value but to inspire people to come together and share. It is like the philosopher's stone: It can transform hatred into love, fear into trust, spiritual hunger into nourishment.

So, it is also with the CODE. By itself, it has no value. But, used by the spiritual misfits of the world, it can bring people to collaborate in the center of a divisive and fragmented village.

The beat of the drum is real.
It echoes throughout history and in all cultures.
It *calls* us to be nourished through sharing with others.

The impulse behind the call has been interpreted through countless symbols, philosophies, and spiritual traditions. When we fail to listen to the beat of the drum, we become stagnant. So, regardless of what you believe or don't believe, and regardless of how you show your love and devotion to family, friends, community, nation, planet, and all that is, your participation in the village matters. Each and every one of us has a role in making the soup delicious. The call to transmute our fear begs us to participate in our own unique ways, not just as individuals (the adults in the story) but as representatives of God as an evolving and complex whole (the village). Each and every one of us counts in this journey—every cell, bacteria, plant, animal, and human. Each of us harbors a perspective that is an essential building block in the unfolding story of God.

A NEW HOPE

I opened by writing, "This book is a more inclusive story of the Universe"—not the only, truest, or best story, but one that is wondrous. It is a story that invites us to believe in the impossible, while simultaneously offering the tools needed to escape contemporary gridlocks.

This story points the way towards many pathways, all of which are worth traveling. It offers a means for coming to know a trillion perspectives of God, and it invites us to ask our most sacred and intimate questions.

It is the *Why not?*
the loosening of rigidity,
an act of maturation.

The story (or myth) of the individual hero's journey has taken us as far as it can. We need a new, collaborative story. The new myth can help us move forward in times of growing complexity and diversity. Because life is a kaleidoscope of holonic and developing perspectives that are inherently rhythmic, balanced, harmonious, and perfect. And life, once again, is changing.

Imagine a religion based on that—
a mythology that can co-exist with our current cosmology,
a faith that promotes universal values,
a psychology that includes awakening,
and awakening that understands development.

This is why the drum beats.
That is why I wrote this book.

My hope is that in the space of true inquiry invited by the CODE, you will begin to reconcile differences and divisions; that where there is separation, you will find unity; that where there is pain, you will discover joy, and where there is joy, you will realize that pain is unavoidable. The CODE is disruptive by nature. It disturbs the status quo. It unmasks us and reveals our vulnerability. It calls us to question 'common sense' and the social conditions of our time. The deeper we go within, the clearer our sight without.

The CODE provides a baseline to get started. This is its contribution. So, go ahead and experiment. Make mistakes. Try the model out and discover if you can learn to fly.

You know this stuff.
It is in your DNA.

The CODE enhances our stories by adding the growing understanding of human development, cultural diversity, and the natural (yet changing) hierarchy of worldviews. The model is a hub for an emerging participatory worldview. It responds to our social complexities, while still taking into consideration personal and cultural perspectives and values.

The metaphor of a soccer game comes to mind. Players are allowed to do whatever they want, as long as they follow the rules of the game and stay on the field. The ground rules of the CODE exist so communities can play this *adaptation game* safely and collaboratively.

The CODE is not intended to change religion. It is simply an orientation that explains the impulse and its evolution through time. It provides a blueprint to explore belonging and collaboration—from grounding to vision building and fruition. The CODE takes into account our current scientific, psychological, and cultural understanding, while staying open to the wisdom of the past and the ideas of tomorrow.

This addresses the problem many spiritual misfits face, allowing them to commit to chosen tradition(s) while holding them lightly. It means that you can live *inside* and *outside* of the religious process so that the great traditions can be integrated with respect, openness, and curiosity in your communities of choice.

As we near the end of this book, I want you to know that I have done my very best to invite you to come to know a new quality of being. I did not intend to provide answers, as I want you to arrive at those on your own, with your community. I know that some of my ideas are raw and unpolished, that they bear the imprint of my background, culture, gender, and life experiences, as well as of many scholars and writers who came before me. I am limited. All perspectives are. And that is the whole point of this book:

I can't do it alone.
No one can do it alone any longer.

Maybe a few of you will take some ideas and run with them. Maybe some will come together and try it out. I know I am.

So, please don't critique the book to point out its drawbacks and my ignorance. That's easy. There are so many. Where would we even begin? Instead, take what you like and throw away the rest. And if you feel the call, I have achieved my goal. If you have not, at least take this:

You are lovable.
You are enough.
You deserve to be treated with kindness and respect.
Your pain matters.
Your life matters.

And...

If my book gave you answers, then forgive me!
Let them go so you can meet your humanity,
that is divine.

BIBLIOGRAPHY

Abram, D. (1996). *The spell of the sensuous: Perception and language in a more than human world.* New York: Vintage books.

Abram, D. (2005). Between the body and the breathing earth: A reply to Ted Toadvine. *Environmental Ethics: An Interdisciplinary Journal Dedicated to The Philosophical Aspects Of Environmental Problems, 27*(2), 171-190.

Abram, D. (2010). *Becoming animal: An earthly cosmology.* New York: Vintage Books.

Adevi, A, A., Grahn, P. (2011). Attachment to Certain Natural Environments: A Basis for Choice of Recreational Settings, Activities and Restoration from Stress? *Environment and Natural Resources Research, 1*(1), 36-52.

Ainsworth, M. (1978). *Patterns of attachment: A psychological study of the strange situation.* Hillsdale, NJ: MDS Lawrence Erlbaum Associates.

Aizenstat, S. (1995) Jungian psychology and the world unconscious. In T. Roszak, M. Gomes, & A. Kanner (Eds.), *Ecopsychology: Restoring the earth, healing the mind* (pp. 92-100). San Francisco, CA: Sierra Club Books.

Alexander, K. B. (2001). *The roots of addiction in free market society.* Vancouver, BC: Canadian Centre for Policy Alternatives.

Alexander, K. B. (2010). *The globalization of addiction: A study in poverty of the spirit.* New York: Oxford University Press.

Alexander, K. B. (2015). Addiction, Environmental Crisis, and Global Capitalism. Retrieved January 2015 from http://www. brucekalexander.com/articles-speeches/ecological-issues/ addiction,-environmental-crisis,-and-global-capitalism

Alford, C. F. (2015). Subjectivity and the intergenerational transmission of historical trauma: Holocaust survivors and their children. Subjectivity, 8(3), 261-282. doi:10.1057/ sub.2015.10

Almaas, A. H. (1988). *The pearl beyond price: Integration of personality into being: An object relations approach.* Berkeley, CA: Diamond Books.

Almaas, A. H. (1996). *The point of existence: Transformations of narcissism in self-realization.* Berkeley, CA: Diamond Books.

American Psychological Association. (2000). *Diagnostic and statistical manual of mental disorders* (4th ed.) (DSM-IV-TR).

Anon. (1971). *The compact edition of the Oxford English Dictionary II.* Oxford and New York: Oxford University Press.

Anodea Judith. (2006). *Eastern body, Western mind.* New-Delhi: Alchemy.

Bai, H. (2012). Reclaiming our moral agency through healing: A call to moral, social, environmental activists, *Journal of Moral Education, 41*(3), 311-327.

Bai, H. & Scutt, G. (2009) Touching the earth with the heart of enlightened mind: The Buddhist practice of mindfulness for environmental education. *Canadian Journal of Environment Education*, 92-106.

Beck, D. E., Cowan, C. (2005). *Spiral Dynamics: Mastering Values, Leadership and Change.* Oxford: Blackwell Business

Beebe, J. (2002). An archetypal model of the self in dialogue. *Theory & Psychology, 12*(2), 267-280.

Biglan, A. (2009). Increasing psychological flexibility to influence cultural evolution. *Behavior and Social Issues, 18,* 15-24.

Binswanger, L. (1941). On the relationship between Husserl's phenomenology and psychological insight. *Philosophy and Phenomenological Research, 2*(2),199-210.

Blackburn. S. (Ed.). (2008) *The Oxford dictionary of philosophy.* Oxford, UK: Oxford University Press. Oxford Reference Online. Oxford University Press. Simon Fraser University. 30 March 2012. Retrieved from: http://www. oxfordreference.com.proxy.lib.sfu.ca/views/ENTRY. html?subview=Main&entry=t98.e182>

Bowlby, J. (1988). *A secure base: Parent-child attachment and healthy human development.* London: Basic Books.

Boyce, B. (2005). Two sciences of the mind. *Shambhala Sun, 13,* 34–43, 93–96.

Brady, K., & Back, S. (2012). Childhood trauma, posttraumatic stress disorder, and alcohol dependence. *Alcohol Research: Current Reviews, 34*(4), 408-413.

Brann, E.T.H. (1991). *The world of the imagination: Sum and substance.* Savage, MD: Rowman & Littlefield.

Brendtro, L. K. (2006). The vision of Uri Bronfenbrenner: Adults who are crazy about kids. Reclaiming children and youth. *The Journal of Strength-based Interventions. 15*(3), 162-166.

Bronfenbrenner, U. (1995). Developmental ecology through

space and time: A future perspective. In P. Moen, G.H. Elder, Jr., & K. Luscher (Eds.), *Examining lives in context: Perspectives on the ecology of human development* (pp. 619-647). Washington, DC: American Psychological Association.

Bronfenbrenner, U. (2005). *Making human beings human: Bioecological perspectives on human development.* Thousand Oaks, CA: Sage.

Carmody, D. L. (1983). *Consciousness and tradition.* By Needleman Jacob. New York: Crossroad, 1982. 173 pages. 14.95. Beyond the Post-Modern Mind. By Smith Huston. New York: Crossroad, 1982. xiii 201 pages. 14.95. Horizons, 10(01), 194–196.

Clark, J. (2008). On being none with nature: Nagarjuna and the ecology of emptiness. *Capitalism, Nature, Socialism, 19*(4), 6-29.

Cleary, J. C. (1986) Trikāya and trinity: The mediation of the absolute. *Buddhist-Christian Studies, 6,* 63-78.

Clinebell, H. (1996). *Ecotherapy: Healing ourselves, healing the earth.* New York: Haworth Press.

Cohen, A., & Bai, H. (2008). Suffering loves and needs company: Buddhist and Daoist perspectives on the counsellor as companion. *Canadian Journal of Counselling, 42*(1), 45-56.

Cohen, A., Bai, H. & Green L. (2008). An experiment in radical pedagogy: Enactment of deep democracy in a philosopher's cafe. *Radical Pedagogy, 9*(2).

Cohen, A. (2009). *Gateway to the Dao-field: Essays for the awakening educator.* Amherst, NY: Cambria Press.

Cohen. A. (2004). Classroom as community: Deep democracy practice, was originally published in 2004 in the *Canadian*

Journal of Counselling (38(3), 152-164) under the title A process-oriented approach to learning process-oriented counselling skills in group.

Collins, M. (2010). Spiritual intelligence: Evolving transpersonal potential toward ecological actualization for a sustainable future. World futures: The *Journal of General Evolution*, 66(5), 320-334.

Connors, J. G., Donovan, M. D., & Diclemente, C. C. (2001). *Substance abuse treatment and the stages of change: Selecting and planning interventions.* New York: Guilford.

De Chardin, P. T. (1976). *The heart of the matter.* Harcourt.

De Chardin, P. T. (2005). *The wings of spirit.* Retrieved from http://ffh.films.com/id/12899/Pierre_Teilhard_de_Chardin_The_Wings_of_Spirit.htm.

Hamilton, M. D. (2013). 'Everything is Workable'. Shambhala.

Dourley, J. (2011). Jung's equation of the ground of being with the ground of psyche. *Journal of Analytical Psychology, 56,* 514–553.

Dowman, K. (2006). *Eye of the storm: Vairotsana's Five Original Transmissions.* Kathmandu, NP: Vara Publications.

Dyer, K. W., Dorahy, M. J., Hamilton, G., Corry, M., Shannon, M., MacSherry, A., & ... McElhill, B. (2009). Anger, aggression, and self-harm in PTSD and complex PTSD. *Journal of Clinical Psychology, 65*(10), 1099-1114.

Edgecombe, R. S. (2002). Keats, Hunt, and soul-making. *Notes & Queries, 49*(1), 37-38.

Edinger, F. E. (1984). *The creation of Consciousness: Jung's myth for modern man.* Toronto, ON: Inner city book.

Edinger, F. E. (1995). *A Journey Through C.G. Jung's Mysterium coniunctionis*. Toronto, ON: Inner City Books.

Eisenstein, C. (2014). How to enslave people with addiction. Retrieved from http://themindunleashed.org/2014/07/enslave-people-addiction.html

Epstein, M. (1999). Beyond the oceanic feeling: Psychoanalytic study of Buddhist mediation. In Molino. A (Ed.), *The couch and the tree: Dialogues in psychoanalysis and Buddhism*. New York, NY: North Point Press.

Epstein, M. (2005). A strange beauty: Emmanuel Ghent and the psychologies of east and west. *Psychoanalytic Dialogues, 15*(2), 125–138.

Epstein. M. (1995). *Thoughts without a thinker*. New York, NY: Basic Book

Esbjörn-Hargens, S., Reams, J., & Gunnlaugson, O. (2010). *Integral education: New directions for higher learning*. Albany, NY: State University of New York Press.

Esbjörn-Hargens, S. (2006). Integral research: A multi-level approach to investigating phenomena. *Constructivism In the Human Sciences, 11*(1), 79-10

Everitt, B. & Heberlein, U. (2013). Current opinion in neurobiology, *Addiction, 23*(4), 463–466.

Fasenfest, D. (2010). Neoliberalism, globalization and the capitalist world order. *Critical Sociology, 36*(5), 627-631.

Fisher, A. (2002). *Radical ecopsychology: Psychology in the service of life*. Albany, NY: State University of New York Press

Flouri, E. (2005). Post-traumatic stress disorder (PTSD). What we have learned and what we still have not found out.

Journal of Interpersonal Violence, 20, 373-379.

Fonagy, P. (2001). *Attachment theory andpPsychoanalysis.* London, UK: Karnac Books. Retrieved from http://www.ebrary.com

Forman, M. D., (2010). A guide to integral psychology: Complexity, integration, and spirituality in practice. New-York: State University of New York Press.

Foster, J. (2011). Therapy without a therapist: Nonduality, healing and the search for wholeness. *Undivided.* Retrieved from http://undividedjournal.com/2011/09/30/therapy-without-a-therapist-nonduality-healing-and-the-search-for-wholeness/

Frattaroli, E. (2002). Healing the soul in the age of the brain: Why medication isn't enough. New York: Viking.

Friedman, M. (1964). Existential psychotherapy and the image of man. *Journal of Humanistic Psychology, 4*(2), 104-117.

Fromme, D. K. (2010). *Systems of psychotherapy: Dialectical tensions and integration.* Springer Science & Business Media.

Gendlin, T. E. (1982). *Focusing.* New York: Bantam

Gil, G. E. (1988). *Outgrowing the pain: A book for and about adults abused as children.* New York: A Dell Trade paperback

Goleman, D. (1981). Buddhist and western psychology: Some commonalities and differences. *Journal of Transpersonal Psychology, 13*(2), 125-136.

Goleman, D. (1993). Psychology, reality and consciousness, In R.Walsh & F. Vaugan (Eds.), *Path beyond ego: The transpersonal vision* (pp. 18-21). New York: Penguin Putnam.

Grange, J. (2011). *Soul: A cosmology.* Albany, NY: State University of New York Press. Retrieved from http://www.ebrary.com

Graves, C. W. (1974). Human Nature Prepares for a Momentous

Leap - Spiral Dynamics. *The Futurist*, 72–87.

Greenspan, M. (2004). *Healing through the dark emotions: The wisdom of grief, fear and despair*. Boston: Shambhala.

Hayes, S. C., & Wilson, K G. (1994). Acceptance and commitment therapy: Altering the verbal support for experiential avoidance. *Behavior Analyst, 17*, 289-303.

Hayes, S. C., Luoma, J., Bond, F., Masuda, A., & Lillis, J. (2006). Acceptance and commitment therapy: Model, processes and outcomes. *Behaviour Research and Therapy, 44*(1), 1–25.

Hiles, D. (2011). *Heuristic inquiry and transpersonal research*. Psychology Department, De Montfort University, Leicester, UK. Retrieved from http://www.psy.dmu.ac.uk/drhiles/HIpaper.htm

Hillman, J. (1972). *The myth of analysis: Three essays in archetypal psychology*. Chicago, Il: Northwestern University.

Hillman, J. (1975). *Re-visioning psychology*. New York: Perennial Library.

Hillman, J. (1982). Anima mundi: The return of the soul to the world. *Spring: A journal of archetype and culture*, 71-79.

Hillman, J. (1997). *The soul code: In searching of character and calling*. New York: Grand-Central Publications.

Hinde, J. (2007). Attachment theory and John Bowlby: Some reflections, *Attachment & Human Development, 9*(4), 337-342.

Hoare, C. (2009). Models of adult development in Bronfenbrenner's bioecological theory and Erikson's biopsychosocial life stage theory: Moving to a more complete three-model view. In M. Smith, N. DeFrates-Densch, M. Smith, & N. DeFrates-Densch (Eds.), *Handbook of research on adult learning and development* (pp. 68-102). New York: Routledge/ Taylor & Francis Group.

Hollis, J. (2005). *Finding meaning in the second half of life: How to finally, really grow up.* NewYork: Penguin.

Hollis, J. (2008). *What matters most: Living a more considered life.* NewYork: Penguin.

Jordan, M. (2009). Nature and self—An ambivalent attachment? *Ecopsychology, 1*(1), 26-31.

Jung, C. G. (1966). The practice of psychotherapy. In RFC Hull (Trans.), *Collected works of C. G. Jung* (Vol. 16). Princeton, NJ: Princeton University Press.

Jung, C. G. (1970). Civilization in transition. In RFC Hull (trans), *Collected works of C. G. Jung (Vol. 10)*. Princeton, NJ: Princeton University Press.

Jung, C. G. (1976). *The symbolic life.* In RFC Hull (Trans.), Collected works of C. G. Jung (Vol. 18). Princeton, NJ: Princeton University Press.

Jung, C. G. (1990a). Archetypes of the collective unconscious. In (1990) Read, H., Fordham, M., & Adler. G., (Eds.). *The Archetypes and the Collective Unconscious.* (pp. 3-41). New York, NY: Bollingen Foundation Inc.

Jung, C. G. (1990b). *Analytical psychology: Its theory and practice.* London: England: Cox & Wyman.

Jung, C. G. (1990c). The significance of the unconscious in psychology. In (1990) Laszlo, V., (Ed.). *The basic writings of Jung* (pp. 39-45).

Jung, C. G. (2002). *The undiscovered self.* London: Routledge press.

Jung. C. G. (1966). What is psychotherapy? In (1966) Read,

H., Fordham, M., & Adler. G., (Eds.). *The practice of psychotherapy: Essays on the psychology of the transference and other subjects* (2nd ed.) (pp. 21- 29). New York, NY: Bollingen Foundation Inc.

Kabat-Zinn, J. (2005). *Wherever you go, there you are: Mindfulness meditation in everyday life.* New York, NY: Hyperion Books.

Keniger, E, L. (2013). What are the benefits of interacting with nature? *International Journal of Environmental Research and Public Health, 10*(3), 913-935.

Kessler, R. (2000). *The soul of education: Helping students find connection, compassion and character at school.* Virginia: Association for Supervision and Curriculum Development.

Kissman, K., & Maurer, L. (2002). East meets west: Therapeutic aspects of spirituality in health, mental health and addiction recovery. *International Social Work, 45*(1), 35-43.

Knight, E. k. (2014). In search of the centaur. *Journal of Integral Theory & Practice, 9*(1), 88-98.

Kornfield, J. (2008). *The wise heart: A guide to the universal teachings of Buddhist psychology.* New York, NY: Bantam Book.

Kotz, M. D. (2002). Globalization and neoliberalism. *Rethinking Marxism, 14*(2), 1-23.

Krishnamurti, J. (1958). *Commentaries on living.* Wheaton, IL: Quest

Krishnamurti, J. (1972). *You are the world: Authentic report of talks and discussions in American universities.* New-York: Krishnamurti Foundation.

Krishnamurti, J. (1974). *On education.* New-York: Krishnamurti Foundation.

Krishnamurti, J. (1975). *The first and last freedom.* New York: Krishnamurti Foundation.

Krishnamurti, J. (1981). *Education and the significance of life.* New York: Krishnamurti Foundation.

Krishnamurti, J. (2004). *Freedom from the known.* Chennai: Krishnamurti foundation

Le Bel, P. (2013). *Becoming intimate with the earth.* Collins Foundation Press: Santa Margarita.

Levine, A. P (2008). *Healing trauma: A pioneering program for restoring the wisdom of your body.* Sounds true (With the CD)

Macy, J. (2007). *World as lover, world as self: Courage for global justice and ecological renewal.* Berkley, CA: Parallax Press.

Magid, B. (2005) *Ordinary mind: Exploring the common ground of Zen and psychoanalysis.* Somerville, MA: Wisdom Publication.

Marchant, F (1992). Anima mundi: Nature poetry. *Harvard Review 1*(1), 28-30.

Martin Buber (2000). *I and Thou.* Ronald Gregor Smith (Translator). Scribner.

May. R. R. (1981). *Freedom and Destiny.* New York: Delta.

McClary, R. (2007). Healing the psyche through music, myth, and ritual. *Psychology of Aesthetics, Creativity, and the Arts, 1*(3), 155-159.

Merleau-Ponty, M. (1962). *Phenomenology of perception.* C. Smith (Trans.). London: Routledge and Kegan Paul.

Mitchell, S. (2005), *Tao Te Ching: The book of the way.* London: Kyle Cathine.

Moon, S. S., Patton, J., & Rao, U. (2010). An ecological approach to understanding youth violence: The mediating role of substance use. *Journal of Human Behavior In The Social Environment, 20*(7), 839-856.

Needleman, J. (1982). *Consciousness and tradition.* New York: Crossroad.

Needleman, J. (1994). *The indestructible question.* London: Penguin Books.

Neufeld, G., & Maté, G. (2005) *Hold on to your kids: Why parents need to matter more than peers.* New York: Ballantine Books.

New York Association for Jungian Analysis. (2008). *About Jungian analysis: Frequently asked questions.* Retrieved February 21, 2011, from http://www.nyaap.org/index.php/id/3/subid/20

Nisargadatta, M. (2005). *I am that: Talks with Sri Nisargadatta Maharaja.* Mumbai: Chetana.

Ogden, P., Minton, K., & Pain, C. (2006). *Trauma and the body: A sensorimotor approach to psychotherapy.* New York: W. W. Norton.

Palmer. P. (2004). *A hidden wholeness: The journey toward an undivided life.* San-Francisco, CA: John Wiley and Sons.

Park, R. S. (2014). *Embodied inner work: An educator's journey of body-mind-heart integration* (Doctoral dissertation). Retrieved from http://summit.sfu.ca/item/14288

Perry, B. (2010). *Working with children to heal interpersonal trauma: The power of play.* (Edited by Eliana Gil with Foreword by Lenore C. Terr., Ed.).

Plotkin, B (2008). *Nature and the human soul: Cultivating wholeness and community in a fragmented world.* New World Library: Novato.

Poole, N., Urquhart, C., Jasiura, F., Smylie, D., Schmidt, R.A., Trauma Informed Practice Project Group, & Trauma Informed Practice Advisory Committee (2013). *Trauma Informed Practice Guide*. Vancouver, BC: British Columbia Centre of Excellence for Women's Health, and British Columbia Ministry of Health.

Prendergast, J, Fenner, P., & Krystal, S. (Eds.). (2003). *The sacred mirror: Non-dual wisdom and psychology* (pp.185-208). St Paul, MN: Paragon House

Pryer, A. (2001) Breaking hearts: Towards an erotics of pedagogy, in Hocking, B., Haskell, J. & Linds, W. (Eds.), *Unfolding bodymind: Exploring possibility through education* (p. 132-). VT: Foundation for Educational Renewal.

Richards, G. (2008). Jung's social psychological meanings. *Journal of Community & Applied Social Psychology, 18*(2), 108-118.

Ringwald, D, C. (2002). The soul of recovery: uncovering the spiritual dimension in the treatment of addictions. New York: Oxford Press.

Rizzuto, A. (1981). *The Birth of the living God*. University of Chicago.

Roberts, B. M (2012). *Re-Connection vs re-collection: Individuation & soul retrieval as remembered wholeness*. Retrieved from http://www.jungcircle.com/ind.html

Roth, F. R. (2005). *The archetype of the holy wedding in alchemy and in the unconscious of modern man*. Retrieved from http://paulijungunusmundus.eu/hknw/holy_wedding_alchemy_modern_man_p1s1_e.htm.

Rundnick, S. (2007). Coming home to wholeness. In C. P. Cooper

(Ed.) *Into the mountain stream: Psychology and Buddhist experience* (pp. 13-25). New-York, NY: Jason Bronson.

Rutzou, T. (2014). Integral theory and the search for the Holy Grail. *Journal of Critical Realism, 13*(1), 77-83.

Ryland, E. (2000). Gaia rising: A jungian look at environmental consciousness and sustainable organizations. *Organization & Environment, 13*(4), 381-402.

Safran, D. (2003). *Psychoanalysis and Buddhism: An unfolding dialogue.* Somerville, MA: Wisdom Publications.

Sally, F. (2002). Ecology of the flesh: Gestalt ontology in Merleau-Ponty and Naess. *International studies in philosophy. 34*(1), 53-67.

Samuels, S., Shorter, B., & Plaut, F. (1993). *A critical dictionary of Jungian analysis.* New York , NY: Routledge.

Schwartz, M. M. (2013). On social holons, ideologies of integral, and the kosmopolitan call of politics. *Journal of Integral Theory & Practice, 8*(3/4), 163-174.

Semetsky, I., & Delpech-Ramey, J. A. (2012). Jung's psychology and Deleuze's philosophy: The unconscious in learning. *Educational Philosophy and Theory, 44*(1), 70-81.

Shafer, I. H. (2002). From noosphere to theosphere: Cyclotrons, cyberspace, and Teilhard's vision of cosmic love. *Zygon: Journal Of Religion & Science, 37*(4), 825-852.

Siegel, D.J. (1999). *The developing mind: How relationships and the brain interact to shape who we are.* New York: Guilford Press.

Siegel, D. J. (2010). *Mindsight: The new science of personal transformation.* New York: Bantam Books.

Siegel, D. J. (2010). Reflections on mind, brain, and relationships in group psychotherapy. *International Journal of Group Psychotherapy, 60*(4), 483-485.

Siegel, D. J. & Solomon, M. (2003) *Healing trauma: attachment, mind, body, and brain.* New York: W. W. Norton & Company.

Singer, J. (1971). *Boundaries of the soul: The practice of Jung's psychology.* New York: Doubleday & Company.

Sleeth, D, B. (2010). Integral love: The role of love in clinical practice as a rite of passage. *Journal of Humanistic Psychology, 50*(4), 471–494.

Staff, A. W (1988). *When society becomes an addict.* California: Harper & Row.

Tarnas, R. (1991). *The passion of the western mind.* New York, NY: Harmony Books.

Tarnas, R. (2002). Is the modern psyche undergoing a rite of passage? *Revision, 24*(3), 2-10.

Theriault, B. (2011). Radical Acceptance: A Non-dual Psychology Approach to Grief and Loss, *International journal of mental health and addiction. 10*(3), 354-367.

United Nations Office on Drugs and Crime. (2010). *Drug statistic and trends.* Vienna: United Nations Office on Drugs and Crime.

Van der Kolk, B. A. (2014). *The body keeps the score: Brain, mind, and body in the healing of trauma.* New York: Viking.

Varela, F., & Thompson E., Rosch, E. (1993), *The embodied mind: cognitive science and human experience.* Massachusetts: MIT Press.

Wallin, D, J. (2007). *Attachment in Psychotherapy,* New York: Guilford Press.

Welwood, J. (2000). *Toward a psychology of awakening: Buddhism, psychology, and the path of personal and spiritual transformation.* Boston, Massachusetts: Shambhala Publications

Wilber, K. (1999). *The collected works of Ken Wilber: The atman project ; Up from Eden.* Shambhala Publications.

Wilber, K. (2000). *Sex, ecology, spirituality.* Boston: Shambhala Publications.

Wilber, K. (2000a). *Integral psychology, consciousness, spirit, psychology.* Boston: Shambhala Publications.

Wilber, K. (2001). *A brief history of everything.* Boston: Shambhala Publications.

Wilber, K. (2006). *Integral spirituality: A startling new role for religion in the modern and postmodern world.* Boston: Shambhala Publications.

Wilber, K. (2017). *The religion of tomorrow.* Boulder: Shambhala

Wilber, K. (2017). Trump and a Post-Truth World. Retrieved from https://www.shambhala.com/trump-and-a-post-truth-world.html

Woodman, M. (1990). *The ravaged bridegroom.* Toronto: Inner City Books.

Woodman, M. (2009). *Dancing in the flames.* Retrieved from http://dancingintheflames.com/Marion_Woodman/HOME.html.

Yalom, J.D. & Leszcz, M. (2005). *The theory and practice of group psychotherapy* (5th Ed.) New York: Basic Books Inc.

Yunt, J. D. (2001). Jung's Contribution to an Ecological Psychology. *Journal of Humanistic Psychology, 41*(2), 96-121.

ENDNOTES

1 I am aware of the limitations of my work, the depth of content and scope of context. I wanted to take you through the history of this emerging movement (starting at the 19th century) and link each idea to its original field. In the end I chose to orient my text more towards future solutions and less about how we got here. As such, this is a very simple commentary on the brilliant thinkers of the past and present. It is a new synthesis of already existing ideas.

2 This is a crude brush stroke of the profound subtleties of cultural and social change that has taken place in the past 400 years, so please excuse me for doing it. I offer some wonderful books in my reference list at the end of the book for anyone who would like to explore more deeply our collective history.

3 Some amazing thinkers are also trying to figure out ways to bridge the gaps of our times. Those I used in the book are referenced and others can be found by a simple Google search.

4 As part of a whole set of psychological goals, the task of individuation stands out as an important one and that is not about to change. Individuation is the archetype of the Hero's journey, the self-actualizing path of soul maturation. This has been the cornerstone of western psychology for more than a decade and spiritual traditions for many centuries. There will always be a need for therapy, self-help books, workshops, and courses that will support both our spiritual aspirations

and the psycho-developmental process. However, what seems to be emerging is a new (yet elemental) longing to find a collaborative voice and vision, that can include the aspiration for autonomy, choice, and freedom but transcend it into belonging.

5 I am paraphrasing the work of the French philosopher François Laruelle, who coined the terms "philosophy without philosophy" and a "non-standard philosophy."

6 Regardless of the topic of interest, only through mastery, over many years of learning and practice, could one begin to taste that depth when one is soaked in the wisdom of a tradition and circles around the religious elements, year after year, to a point where it becomes part of who one is.

7 Theory will be introduced throughout the book but I would like you to see it as a by-product, not the essence.

8 A holon is something that is simultaneously a whole and a part. The word was coined by Arthur Koestler in his book *The Ghost in the Machine* (1967, p. 48) but was popularized by Ken Wilber in his breakthrough book *Sex, Ecology and Spirituality*.

9 Not anything you might define as love. Once again, I ask that you assume we don't speak the same language.

10 "The very condition that modern rational consciousness would dissuade us from — personifying — returns in our relationships, creating an animistic world of personified idols." (Hillman, 1975, p. 47)

11 Needleman writes: "The academic effort to arrive at a single satisfactory definition of religion is bound to fail, not because there is no common essence to all great religions of the world, but because the practices and teaching of the various religions have in the recent past been examined with the part of the mind that divides and analyzes, rather than the hidden part of the mind that can perceive, through its own need, the unity which underlies an outer diversity." (Needleman, 1982, p. 37)

12 I promise to make this point much clearer in Part two.

13 I will bring many examples in Part two of the book.

14 Pew Research Forum. Retrieved from: http://www.pewforum. org/2015/04/02/religious-projections-2010-2050

15 Pearson, Janz & Ali (2013) write: "In 2012, a total of 2.8 million Canadians aged 15 and older, or 10.1%, reported symptoms consistent with at least one of the following mental or substance use disorders: major depressive episode, bipolar disorder, generalized anxiety disorder, and abuse of or dependence on alcohol, cannabis or other drugs. Over the course of a lifetime, rates of substance use disorders were higher than the rates for mood disorders. About six million Canadians met the criteria for substance use disorder, while 3.5 million met the criteria for mood disorder." (p. 1)

16 Brené Brown writes: "Over half of the participants who talked about experiencing shame in their faith history, also found resilience and healing through spirituality. The majority of them changed their churches and beliefs but spirituality and faith remind important part of their life... They believed that the sources of shame arouse from the earthly, man-made, human interrupted rules and regulations and the social community expectations of religion, rather than their personal relationship with God or the divine. Our faith narrative must be protected and we must remember that no person is ordained to judge our divinity or to write the story of our spiritual worthiness." (*Brené Brown, Rising Strong*).

17 From "The Buried Life" (1852), st. 2 by Matthew Arnold.

18 Religions are often boxed into narrow perspectives, which are apparent in comments such as: I don't believe in your God. (What God don't you believe in?). If you are religious, you believe in heaven and hell. (Define those terms). How can someone with so much education be religious? (Why do we have this assumption?). You will try to convert

me! (From what to what?). I must think for myself! (Who told you you can't?). Science and religion don't mix. (They don't and they can). With such beliefs we miss not only the diverse nature of reality but also the developmental qualities of the impulse.

19 *The Religions of Tomorrow* is a comprehensive reference for anyone who is feeling the call to adapt and grow. Wilber does a really good job in explaining his theory in a religious context, something I was not planning to do in this book. It is a must read for anyone who is interested in the evolution of religion and God. The book you are reading can be understood as a commentary on his life work. It is not as extensive as what Wilber mapped in "Religions of tomorrow," but it does dialogue with some of his ideas.

20 Sixty-five percent of North Americans take prescription medications daily, 43% take mood altering prescriptions regularly. There were more than 3.3 billion prescriptions filled in America in 2002 (12 times the U.S. population; that's 12 prescriptions for every man, woman, and child in the U.S. that year).Posttraumatic Stress Disorder: 7.7 million, 3.5%; Research published in The American Journal of Psychiatry found that major depression rates for American adults increased from 3.33 percent to 7.06 percent from 1991 through 2002. Depression is also considered a worldwide epidemic, with five percent of the global population suffering from the condition, according to the World Health Organization:

21 Source: http://www.worldometers.info/

22 Source: https://www.cigna.com/. Cigna has conducted a massive study on loneliness.

23 Source: https://www.cigna.com/

24 Source: https://www.cigna.com/

25 A hundred years after the United States began its war on alcohol usage, more and more people in North America (and around the world)

are suffering from some sort of addiction—and the numbers speak for themselves. From the United Nations Office on Drugs and Crime, (2010): Number of people who inject drugs aged 15-64—11 to 21 million. Number of "problem drug users" aged 15-64—16 to 38 million. Number of people who have used drugs at least once in the past year aged 15-64—155 to 250 million (p. 123). And these numbers refer only to alcohol and drug issues. They do not cover other forms of addiction with which so many are dealing.

26 Dislocation is the lack or loss of psychosocial integration in one person or, in some cases, within society (Alexander 2010).

27 Dr. Fred Alford, Professor emeritus at the University of Maryland, (2015) adds: "The communal body is made up of attachments to a place as much as human attachments. When the place disappears, so does the bond connecting the individual to the world... treatment aim is to restore the individual's connection between the individual and their community."

28 I am not blind to the theories and ideologies that offer their own version of comprehensive solution. I just don't believe they are really comprehensive...

29 And just to be clear, these are behaviors that are in line with the law and where people don't get physically hurt. Empathy does not mean that one becomes a doormat or that one approves dangerous or lawless behaviors.

30 Just a quick note—many religious or political organizations also have a direction but lack the understanding of developmental worldview and emerging perspectives.

31 This term comes from Acceptance and Commitment therapy.

32 I encourage communities to engage in long-term trainings over the years so when members finish the seven years, they have a whole set of

skills and education to becomes leaders of their own communities or in the tribe as it transitions into the next seven-year cycle.

33 I use the term *tribal* because it is the smallest structure that is bigger than an extended family, and because it reminds me of how we used to live. However, if you don't like the word tribe, come up with something that will work for you and your community.

34 I predict that eventually, these second-tier tribes will collaborate with one another and gather to create greater formations.

35 For more information, please read "The theory and practice of group psychotherapy" by Irvin D. Yalom. It is considered one of the most comprehensive books on group facilitation and can be a very important resource for the leadership team. "Everything is Workable" by Diane Musho Hamilton is another practical book on resolving conflict resolution. I mention only two books here but there are so many great resources that can save you a lot of grief.

36 Please use already established tools and therapy to achieve this (e.g., nonviolent communication, the writings of Brené Brown and Byron Katie, and so on).

37 The Emotional-sensual "body." Our moving, gushing, intelligent energy. We learn to explore our emotional life and grow our capacity to have healthy transactions with others and with oneself, which is the ability to stay present and grounded even with difficult emotions arise. Emotional literacy enriches our human experience by orienting us back to ourselves. It also puts words into what can be a very fluid, and of course also difficult, experience.
- The Mind. While worldviews tend to be rigid, and have a harder time adjusting to change, a "yes, no and maybe..." approach, that is based on the principle of balance can help us learn the art of making sense of an increasingly paradoxical world. It teaches people to see others without the fear of losing themselves. It's an essential principle in embracing our own limitations, drawbacks and inabilities.

- Being, or spirit is where we are already awake and free. Learning to rest as the nature of the mind is how to tap into this body.

- The Physical, or somatic "body" will include embodied insights, somatic awareness, trauma relief, chemical and hormonal balance.

- The Soul making body has sprouted in consciousness, the psyche begins its transformation into becoming more than what once was believed the self is. This is established through the cultivation of inner diversity and multiplicity, which involves a slow eradication of false attachment to our identities and social masks and the decentralization of the psychic life.

38 Krishnamurti writes, "The observer and the observed are one; the thinker and his thoughts are one. To experience the thinker and his thought as one is very arduous for the thinker is ever taking shelter behind his thought; he separates himself from his thoughts to safeguard himself, to give himself continuity, permanency; he modifies or changes his thoughts, but he remains." (J. Krishnamurti, Ojai, California. 6th Public Talk, 1946)

ABOUT THE AUTHOR

Shahar Rabi, Ph.D., is an Assistant Professor of Counselling Psychology at Adler University. He formerly served as the Clinical Program Director at the Orchard Recovery Centre. He has years of experience in treating addiction, trauma, depression, and anxiety. He is also the Co-Founder of the New Earth Institute in Vancouver. Shahar has a broad spectrum of work experience as a choreographer, philosopher and yoga teacher, meditation instructor, and even as a clown. As a clinician, he draws on years of formal studies at universities in Israel and Canada, as well as practice with prominent non-dual teachers in India, Nepal, Thailand, and Israel. He lives on the West Coast of Canada with his wife and two children and can frequently be found on the forest and mountain trails of the island he calls home.

For more information,
please visit

www.newearthinstitute.com

NOTES

N O T E S

N O T E S

Made in the
USA
Middletown, DE